ORKNEY

PATRICK BAILEY

PEVENSEY
ISLAND GUIDES

For
Friends in Orkney

All photographs and drawings are by
the author unless otherwise
acknowledged. Andrzej Kuhn's painting
Vikings (title page) is reproduced by
permission of the artist and of the
Goldmark Gallery in Uppingham.

The Pevensey Press is an imprint of
David & Charles

Map on page 6 by Ethan Danielson

ISBN 0 907115 99 3 (hardback)
ISBN 0 907115 93 4 (paperback)

Designed and typeset by
Drum & Company
and printed in Hong Kong
by Wing King Tong Co Ltd
for David & Charles
Brunel House
Newton Abbot   Devon

ORKNEY

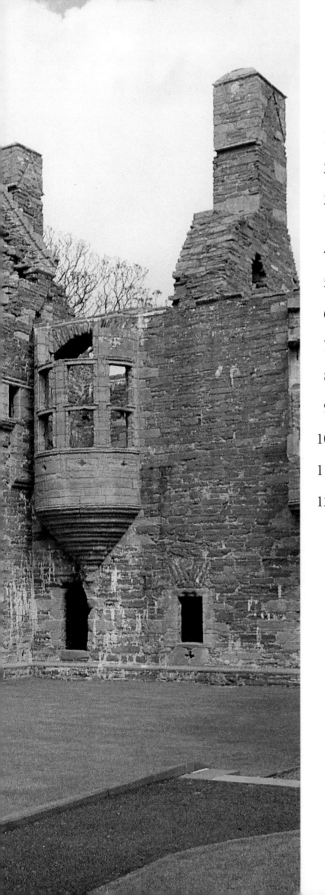

Contents

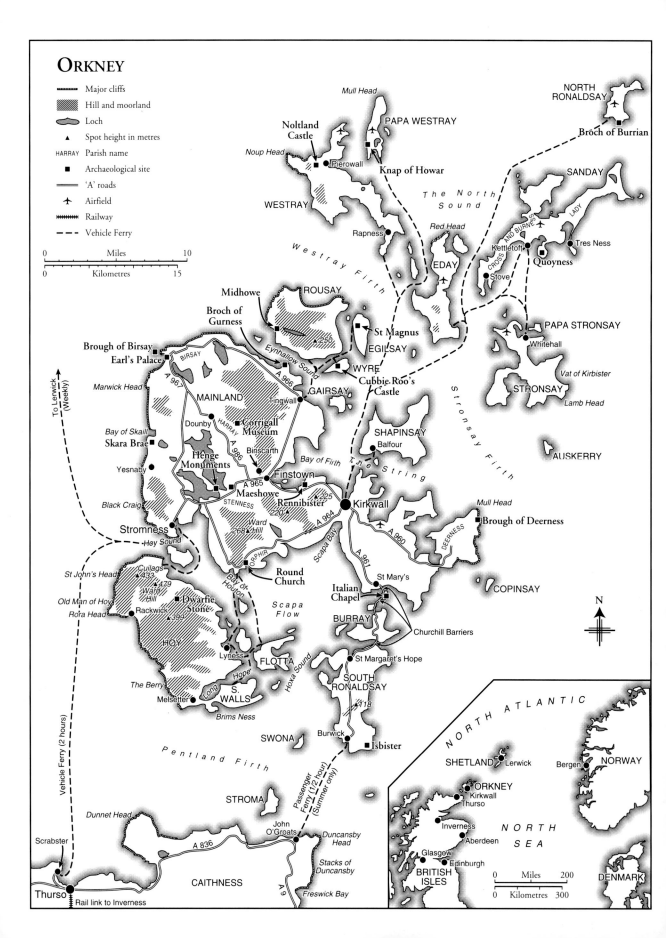

ORKNEY

- ····· Major cliffs
- ▨ Hill and moorland
- ⬮ Loch
- ▲ Spot height in metres
- HARRAY Parish name
- ■ Archaeological site
- ══ 'A' roads
- ✈ Airfield
- ┿┿┿ Railway
- ─ ─ Vehicle Ferry

Miles 0 — 10
Kilometres 0 — 15

1 THE PERSONALITY OF ORKNEY

'ARE THEY PART OF THE HEBRIDES?' 'Do the people speak Gaelic?' 'Which is Orkney, which is Shetland?' These questions are often asked by people who are thinking of visiting the Northern Isles for the first time. The answers are, of course, 'No', 'No', and 'Orkney is nearest to Scotland'. The sixty-seven islands which make up the Orkney archipelago, of which sixteen are inhabited, lie immediately off the coast of Caithness, the fertile north-east corner of the Scottish mainland from which they are separated by the stormy Pentland Firth. Shetland lies much further out, a full 56 miles (90km) beyond North Ronaldsay, Orkney's farthest island. However, historically, geologically and in every other way, these northern island groups have little to do with the Hebrides: since the eighth century, Orkney's links have been first with Scandinavia, then with lowland Scotland. For more than five centuries the islands formed part of the sea empire of the north founded by Norwegian kings and settled by people who came westwards from the overcrowded fiords. Only in 1468 did Orkney become part of Scotland; consequently Gaelic is unknown in Orkney.

Above: Stromness, Orkney's second town, overlooking the sheltered haven of Hamla Voe

Patterns in Orkney flagstone. Long ago, this rock was mud on the bed of a great lake, gradually drying up under desert conditions

Granite boulders in a Stromness wall. Orkney's oldest rocks, which contain uranium, are found nearby

Laminations: layer upon layer of Old Red Sandstone exposed on an Orkney shore

'Is Orkney rocky and mountainous, like the Hebrides?' 'Isn't the weather appalling?' 'Surely it's dark most of the time in winter?' These questions also arise frequently, and it may be a good idea to correct, right from the start, the false impressions that have inspired them. Orkney is never rugged, like Harris and parts of Lewis. It is fertile and populous, with more than 19,000 people; a land of cultivated fields, beef cattle (at least 100,000) and dairy herds; a green country overlooked by low, rounded hills covered with heather and grass. Some of the hills offer fine walking, particularly in Hoy.

Geologically, Orkney is an extension of the Caithness lowlands. The islands' characteristic rocks are flagstones, reddish, ochre and brown in colour, and closely allied to the red rocks of Devon and Herefordshire. Some of the flagstones make excellent building material, which is one reason why Orkney has so many well-preserved ancient monuments. The flagstones are of two distinct ages: the newer and more massive form the striking Hoy hills, the backdrop to most distant views in Orkney – the name 'Hoy' derives, in fact, from the Old Norse for 'high island'; the older flagstones form the less dramatic hills and lowlands of Mainland and the other islands. Only behind Stromness do really ancient rocks appear, peeping up through the flagstones to form Brinkie's Brae and a ridge of stony hills. These are part of the deep foundations of Europe and in Orkney they contain uranium. In the early days of nuclear power when fuel was thought to be in short supply, there were official proposals to extract these rocks, making a huge hole in the process. Fortunately other sources were found and the proposals were shelved.

Within the last million years or so, in what scientists refer to as recent geological time, Orkney was overrun by moving ice which smoothed the hills and gouged out deep hollows and valleys; now that sea-level has risen again, these form lochs and sea-channels. The ice also deposited the muds, sands, clays and gravels which are the basis of Orkney's soils. These soils are often boggy, and so drainage has always been a pre-occupation with Orkney farmers.

As to Orcadian weather, this certainly can be appalling, although usually it is not. There can be days of gales, driving rain and an overall bleakness which is daunting to residents and visitors alike, but equally there can be wonderfully clear days with marvellous visibility and a great sense of space. Cloud effects can be magnificent at any time of the year, and the northern light has a crystal-clear quality which is unknown in the south.

Midsummer sunset, Loch of Stenness

Right: twenty-to-midnight, June, Bay of Firth

Previous page: dramatic coasts. Light and shadow on the Mainland coast at Yesnaby

Summer days seem endless. On the longest day the sun hardly sinks below the horizon, and according to tradition it is perfectly possible to play golf or read *The Times* or *The Orcadian* (Orkney's local newspaper) at midnight out of doors. In practice, however, following the ball is none too easy and it is difficult to read the small print.

Because of Orkney's high latitude, winter nights are long. The islands lie as far north as St Petersburg or Churchill on Hudson Bay and are a mere 50 miles (80km) south of Greenland's Cape Farewell. In December the sun does not rise until after 9am and sets soon after 3pm, and if the weather is cloudy there is little light at any time. It is not, however, very cold: the warm Atlantic waters and the winds which constantly blow from the west keep Orkney free of frost in most years, and snow rarely lies for long, except on the Hoy hills. January temperatures at sea-level are about the same as those for the Kent and Sussex coasts, 4–6°C.

Fine winter days can be the most memorable of all in Orkney. Hills are brown and purple with heather, and Hoy is powdered with snow, dazzlingly white and clean; the colours of the sounds and sea-channels reminiscent of Homer's wine-dark sea. Unfortunately few visitors ever see Orkney in its magnificent winter apparel.

Orkney's coastline is its greatest scenic glory, as the ceaseless pounding of Atlantic waves has sculpted its sandstone cliffs into spectacular shapes. On the west coast of Mainland, around Yesnaby for instance, there is a quite extraordinary array of sea-stacks, caves, natural arches, blow-holes (called gloups) and the narrow, trench-like inlets called geos (pronounced gews). Here, too, are broad bays with beaches and sand-dunes; at the Bay of Skaill, dunes have preserved one of Europe's most celebrated archaeological sites, Skara Brae.

Away from the Atlantic furies the coasts are mostly low-lying, with broad, curving bays, sheltered channels and vistas of low, rounded hills. The Atlantic cliffs are home to more than a million seabirds, and the lowland coasts attract seals, otters, dolphins and sometimes whales.

Atlantic breakers pounding an Orkney shore

ORKNEY'S FIRST PEOPLES

THE FIRST PEOPLE followed the retreating ice into Orkney. Sea-level was slowly rising, giving the islands their present outlines, yet some of these first people probably walked across a land-bridge from Caithness; others would have come by boat. They made their homes on Orkney's best land, usually within easy reach of the sea or a freshwater loch, and have left us a magnificent array of prehistoric monuments – but no written records. Possibly they spoke a form of Gaelic, we simply do not know. These First Orcadians lived in Orkney for very much longer than Anglo-Saxon peoples have so far lived in Britain; and then, mysteriously, they seem to have faded away – or did they? Their apparent disappearance is one of the great puzzles of Orkney's early history.

In the ninth century of our era – we do not know exactly when – new groups of settlers from the east began to land in Orkney each summer. They were part of the great Scandinavian expansion around the North Atlantic margins, an expansion which took intrepid voyagers to the northern isles of Scotland, to Faroe, to Iceland, Greenland and finally to Vinland, which today we call Labrador. Orkney offered the Norse colonists a fertile and secure base close to the Scottish coast (though Scotland had yet to become one country). Accordingly the islands became the headquarters of a Norse earldom, and Kirkwall, its capital, grew to be the only Norse-age town of any significance in Britain.

Historic Orkney: Kirkwall, the capital, once the foremost town in the Norse commercial empire of the north

Unlike the First Orcadians, these Norse settlers *have* left us an account of their doings in the form of the *Orkneyinga Saga*, a fascinating series of stories available in modern editions. The *Saga* stories were first recited, then written down by an unknown author in Iceland in the twelfth century. However, when telling the story of the settlement and the foundation of the earldom, the *Saga* makes no mention of any other people living in Orkney before the Norse colonists arrived: not being Norse, they could have no part in stories about Norse heroes.

The Norse occupation of Orkney was extremely thorough. Almost every ancient place-name is Old Norse in origin, and if there were any First Orcadian place-names, none have survived for certain. For many centuries a version of Old Norse called the Orkney Norn was spoken in the islands, but it died out about two centuries ago. All the Orkney dialects – and there was one for every island and for all the major sectors of Mainland – are shot through with Norse words and turns of speech, though unhappily these dialects are becoming less distinct as a result of television and education. The telephone book contains many Norse family names, slightly Scotticised. It is interesting, too, that Kirkwall's ancient core looks very much as though it had been planned in Norway and built in Orkney from local materials. Its cathedral, Orkney's finest building, is dedicated to a Norse earl mentioned in the *Saga* and another Norse earl was its founder.

Left: the great 'geo' or wave-cut inlet, Windwick

FROM THE *SAGA* TO MODERN TIMES

THE NORWEGIAN sea empire was always precarious. It depended upon long sea crossings in high latitudes which were hard to maintain, especially in winter. It is not surprising therefore to find that the generations of Orkney people who grew up after the conquest soon began to lose touch with their origins, and to be drawn more and more into the affairs of an emergent Scotland.

The last Norwegian king to try to re-assert his power in the Scottish north came to Orkney in 1263 and died in Kirkwall the following winter after a disastrous campaign. Afterwards, all the earls of Orkney were Scots, though theoretically they remained tributary to the kings of Norway. Gradually the political realities of the situation asserted themselves, as they always do; and in 1468 the Orkney earldom was ceded to the Crown of Scotland by a Danish king who had inherited the Norse dominions. Soon after the union the earldom came to a stormy conclusion, and Orkney became a remote and little regarded province of Scotland. There followed a kind of pause in Orkney's history in which few events of note seemed to happen.

This timeless period was ended decisively by the Napoleonic wars. Once again the sea-lanes were busy and so Orkney began to prosper and to feel the influence of the world outside. Then came the twentieth century, and

Ruined crofts in South Ronaldsay, abandoned between the two world wars

Reminders of war: a blockship sunk in 1940 to stop U-boats entering Scapa Flow

with it the events of two world wars, the discovery of North Sea oil and the rise of the tourist industry. The wars and the oil brought Orkney back into the mainstream of politics and commerce, at least for the time being.

Today, however, as the last years of this century run their course, there are fears in Orkney that these islands, like others located around the margins of Europe, may be moving into a time of increasing disadvantage. This is largely because they are far removed from the places where decisions are made, in Britain, in Europe and in the wider world.

In the following chapters, Orkney's many and varied attractions will be explored, and places to visit will be suggested. But first, how does one reach Orkney?

TRAVELLING TO ORKNEY
AND MOVING AROUND

FERRIES

Daily all-the-year-round vehicle and passenger ferries cross the Pentland Firth to Kirkwall and Stromness from Invergordon (Orcargo) and Scrabster (P & O Ferries). From May to September there is a passenger ferry from John O'Groats to Burwick in South Ronald-say (Thomas & Bews); it is intended to make this latter ferry a ro-ro.

FLIGHTS

Two airlines serve Orkney: British Airways flies from Heathrow, Birmingham, Belfast, Manchester, Glasgow, Edinburgh and Aberdeen to Kirkwall daily during the week; Loganair uses smaller aircraft and provides a week-day service from Edinburgh, Glasgow and Wick. The flight from Wick takes about ten minutes and may suit those many people who dislike flying. It also offers fine views of the Caithness coast around Duncansby Head and Scapa Flow. Cars may be left at Wick airfield. In summer, Loganair also provides a weekly service to Bergen.

A cultivated regular landscape. Beef cattle farms in Mainland seen from the air

TRAVELLING TO ORKNEY

There are several ways of reaching Orkney from the south, and all have their advantages. For those who have time, the drive through Scotland to the north coast is to be strongly recommended; many interesting diver-

Depopulation: the remote community of Rackwick on Hoy's Atlantic coast is abandoned, except for some holiday homes

sions are possible, serving as introduction to the Orkney experience. For example, between Edinburgh and Inverness you might go in search of the many fine Pictish symbol stones which lie within easy reach of the A9. Orkney has yielded six good examples of such carved stones, and in the pre-Norse period there can be no doubt that the islands formed part of the Pictish dominions.

North of Inverness another diversion can be made to Dornoch Firth to explore the area where one of the first earls mentioned in the *Saga* lies buried. This was Sigurd the Mighty who extended Norse power far south into Scotland; he died of blood-poisoning after battle somewhere near Bonar Bridge in 875. The *Saga* says he was 'howe-laid' hereabouts, though nobody knows exactly where – a clue is perhaps offered by the farm named Sydera, which could possibly mean 'Sigurd's Howe'. A ramble over the picturesque glacial ridges called 'eskers' behind the farm can evoke plenty of guesses about where the howe of a great chief may have been built. Incidentally, soon after the last war some Norwegian amateur archaeologists came to Sydera to look for Sigurd's howe and at one stage thought they had found it – but on closer inspection the buried structures turned out to be a Home Guard dugout from the 1940s!

North of Dornoch Firth you could choose not to take the main coast road to Thurso and the Scrabster ferry, but to make a foray north-westwards into the wilds of Sutherland, travelling via Bonar Bridge, Lairg and Altnaharra to reach the coast below Ben Hope. A well-preserved Iron Age broch stands beside this route, a foretaste of Orkney where brochs were probably invented. Sutherland was the great southern barrier land which cut off *Saga*-age Orcadians from Scotland, its rocky terrain contrasting dramatically with the fertility of Caithness and the islands beyond.

The ferry voyage from Scrabster to Stromness is spectacular. In fine weather the vessel sails along the Atlantic coast of Hoy, giving fine views of the Old Man of Hoy, Britain's tallest sea-stack, and the giant cliffs of St John's Head. On rough days the ferry takes a more protected route through Scapa Flow, passing Lyness with its Napoleonic martello towers and wartime installations and giving distant views of Flotta, Orkney's oil island away to the east. Both routes converge on Stromness, surely one of the most picturesque small towns in Scotland.

TRAVELLING IN ORKNEY

THE ISLES other than Mainland, Orkney's principal island, may be reached by Orkney Islands Shipping Company ferries and by Loganair internal flights. Boats may be hired for particular inter-island trips, and boat excursions are frequently advertised.

Where shelter can be found from the wind, gardens grow. A fine private garden in St Ola near Kirkwall

All the islands have an excellent road network. Local bus services do exist, but it is difficult to move around without one's own transport. Cars and bicycles may however be hired, although it is advisable to do this in advance during the main holiday season.

The Orkney Tourist Board should be consulted for up-to-date information and advice about travel and accommodation. Its numerous leaflets and other publications, including a substantial islands *Handbook*, contain details regarding ferries and air services, catering facilities, access to ancient monuments, the hire of cars, bicycles and boats and all types of accommodation: hotels and guest-houses, bed-and-breakfast, cottages for hire, camping and youth hostel facilities, and so on. The dates and times of forthcoming events, of which there are always a large number, may also be obtained from the Tourist Board. The events of a typical year are likely to include concerts, conferences, art exhibitions, a science festival, films, theatrical productions, discos. St Magnus' Festival of music and drama takes place in midsummer, Stromness Shopping Week is held in July, the Kirkwall Agricultural Show takes place in early August. Those who can visit Orkney at Christmas and New Year may also witness the extraordinary Ba' Game, played by several hundred people along Kirkwall's main street. Few 'ferry loupers' (outside visitors) ever see this event.

The Tourist Board is a highly efficient organisation, with offices in central Kirkwall and at Stromness pierhead. The weekly *Orcadian* newspaper is another invaluable source of up-to-the-minute information; it can be obtained through the post.

Having arrived in Orkney, Kirkwall is perhaps the best place for the visitor to see first because it brings together so many strands of Orkney history.

These two pictures show William Daniell's view of Kirkwall as it appeared in 1818. His first viewpoint is the Ayre or shingle bank which now carries the main road from Kirkwall to Stromness. The Peerie Sea, still being used by small fishing boats, is foreground to cathedral, castle, palaces and the single street

Daniell's second viewpoint shows St Magnus' Cathedral from the south-east, approximately the site of the modern British Telecom building. The ruined Earl's Palace is to the left of the cathedral with the tower of the Bishop's Palace just visible beyond. In the foreground is a good crop of bere, the ancient variety of barley which ripens early in the north

2 KIRKWALL THE CAPITAL

THE ANCIENT TOWN OF KIRKWALL came into being in Norse times and grew rapidly to become the largest town in the northern isles. In 1486, soon after the union with Scotland, King James III granted it the status of a royal burgh; this effectively gave the town a monopoly over all trade in the islands. The shape of this original town is now embedded within a much larger, built-up area. The original layout shows up clearly in the earliest-known picture of Kirkwall, an inset on the *Estate of Grain* map of 1766. We may also see it in William Daniell's aquatints of the town, drawn in about 1815 and published in the 1820s.

A good place from which to begin unscrambling the town's layout is Kirk Green, the open space in front of St Magnus' Cathedral. Here we are at the heart of the Laverock, the earls' and bishops' town and for centuries the centre of power in the islands. Kirk Green looks like a marketplace and in fact it used to be the site of the Lammas Fair, held for three days in the first week in August. Hundreds of stalls would be erected on the open space and along what is today Palace Road, and the whole area would be thronged with a multitude of people from all the islands and from across the Pentland Firth. Like all fairs, this was just as much a social as a commercial occasion, a time when marriages were arranged and deals done about land, property and politics.

Beyond the ancient buildings which face St Magnus' across Kirk Green, and the newer buildings which stand behind them, is the Peerie or Little Sea, a tidal inlet which was Kirkwall's first harbour. Possibly there were once small piers along the shore of this sea, as there are today along the shore at Stromness, but no trace of them remains. The Peerie Sea was sheltered naturally by a sandbar called the Ayre, but before long ships became too large to use the inlet and in the nineteenth century it was sealed off by a causeway

The earliest-known picture of Kirkwall, found as an inset on the Estate of Grain *map of 1766. It shows the medieval town's single street, the ruined Sinclair castle, St Magnus' Cathedral and the two palaces lining the shore of the Peerie Sea* (Courtesy of Orkney County Library)

Kirk Green, Kirkwall's ancient marketplace in front of St Magnus' Cathedral. To the left is Tankerness House, now a museum but formerly the home of an important Orkney commercial family

'The street', Kirkwall's main thoroughfare, recently pedestrianised for part of its length

which carried the new road west towards Stromness. Once enclosed, the former harbour was partly filled in and a new, lower section of the town was built on it. It also became the unsavoury receptacle for town rubbish. However, in recent times the Peerie Sea has been cleaned up and the area around it landscaped so that it once more gives a pleasing frontage to the town.

Old Kirkwall consists of one long, irregular street more than a kilometre long which follows the original shore of the Peerie Sea. It has five different names, all of them quite modern: in Kirk Green it is called Broad Street, then towards the harbour it becomes first Albert Street, then Bridge Street; away from the harbour it is first Victoria Street, then Main Street. The whole length of the street is paved as though it had been pedestrianised, though in fact traffic is allowed along most of it. Pedestrianisation has been discussed for at least thirty years and was first tried as an experiment in 1994 in Albert Street only.

At the north end of Kirk Green the junction of Albert and Castle Streets marks the location of Kirkwall Castle, now demolished. This castle was built in the shadowy time when the earls were Scots but the Norwegians still ruled. Earl Henry Sinclair built it to secure his effective independence when there was still a chance that a King of Norway might return, and no chance at all that the Scots would still be able to do anything to help the earl

'The street' showing the Big Tree, now sadly diminished. For many years this was Orkney's largest tree, owing its size to shelter from the town's buildings

if he did so. Only once was the Sinclair castle besieged, in 1614 in the dying days of the earldom when the last earl and his son unwisely rebelled against King James VI of Scotland and paid the penalty with their heads. Soon afterwards the castle was partly dismantled. Its ruins remained an obstruction to the development of Kirkwall until 1865 when it was completely cleared away. Some of its stones were used to build Kirkwall town hall in 1884. Today there are no visible remains of the castle, only fragments of its foundations in the cellars of houses on the site.

A short way beyond the castle site stands the 'Big Tree', said to have been the largest tree in Orkney. It owed its size to the protection of the town's buildings – in Orkney, walls and buildings shelter trees, and not the other way around. According to legend, Mr Gladstone, who was an enthusiastic tree-feller, wished to cut the Big Tree down when he visited Orkney; so railings were quickly put round it to dissuade him!

Several narrow passages and streets lead off Albert Street, some lined with picturesque buildings. In one of these, Laing Street, is Orkney Public Library; its Orkney Room contains a comprehensive and unique collection of books and other source-materials relating to virtually every aspect of the islands' development, including a sound archive. After World War II, this library pioneered a book-box service to isolated communities throughout Orkney. It plays a very important part in the cultural life of the islands.

At the top of Laing Street and a short distance to the right stand the nineteenth-century buildings which for many years housed Kirkwall Grammar School, or KGS as it has always been referred to; the buildings are now the offices of the county education authority. The origins of KGS are closely associated with the building of St Magnus' Cathedral: the school's founder is thought to have been Bishop Bjarni, one of Orkney's most scholarly and practical bishops and a contemporary and friend of Earl Rognvald, the cathedral's founder. The earl endowed the school with farms in the island of Sanday, ensuring its continuance through the centuries. Bjarni's school probably stood near the foot of what is today Palace Road. In 1764 it was transferred to larger buildings on Kirk Green; and then in 1820, by which time the Burgh Council had gained full control of the school from the church, it was moved to this site on the hill just east of the cathedral. After

World War II these buildings too were found inadequate; and so KGS, by now a comprehensive school, was transferred to a new educational complex in Papdale valley where it stands today.

This is a suitable point at which to note the traditional excellence of Orkney's schools. Over the centuries, many notable men and women have received their schooling at KGS. Considering the small population of the islands, a truly remarkable number have gone on to universities in Scotland and to a wide variety of distinguished national and international careers. This high educational quality continues. In 1993, for example, the Scottish Office published its three-year survey of Scottish schools' examination achievements which revealed that the schools in Orkney and Shetland had achieved a higher percentage of top grades in the Standard grade and Highers examinations than the schools of any other Scots county. These are the main university entrance examinations in Scotland, taken at the age of sixteen. Such scholastic honours tell only part of the educational story in a comprehensive school, but they do reflect great credit on all those responsible for education in the islands, including the students. It is no mean feat to provide an education of this quality at the farthest edges of Britain.

Fragment of St Olav's church built into a modern wall. St Olav's gave Kirkwall its name of 'Church Bay'

Beyond Laing Street, the Kirkwall 'main street' takes a turn to the left and crosses a piped stream, the Papdale Burn; this now-invisible stream gives the name to Bridge Street. A narrow passage to the right leads to the site of St Olav's church, the original Norse church which gave the name 'Church Bay' to Kirkwall. A tiny fragment of archway has been built into a modern wall, otherwise nothing remains of this church which became redundant when St Magnus' Cathedral was built. Bridge Street ends at Kirkwall's modern harbour; this was originally planned by Thomas Telford, as were so many harbours in the north. Kirkwall's largest hotels face the harbour, reminiscent of the fact that until recently most of their guests came by sea.

Most of the shops and the professional and administrative offices have frontages on the 'main street' between Kirk Green and the harbour. The town has not yet suffered the full effects of the supermarket revolution, so its shops are often individual and interesting, and well worth a closer look.

Returning to Kirk Green and looking left or south, the most important building in view is Tankerness House, now a museum. This fine house started life as a cathedral property; its present appearance dates from 1574. Its survival as an important feature of Kirkwall's townscape was due to the cathedral's last archdeacon, Gilbert Foultie, who at the Reformation managed to secure the building, which he had occupied in his ecclesiastical capacity, and make it his private dwelling. Later it became the home of the Baikie family, landowners and merchant venturers and key figures in the commercial development of the town. Tankerness House is a splendid museum of Orkney life through the ages. The walled garden behind it is also a delight, and a reminder of what can be done with a garden, even in Orkney, when adequately sheltered from the wind.

The main street continues south as Victoria Street and is well worth exploring, though it has few shops. While few, if any, of its buildings are of particular architectural merit, the overall effect of the street is balanced and pleasing. Would that modern town streets were so unpretentiously good to look at!

Tankerness House, once a cathedral property, later the town house of the Baikie family and now a museum of Orkney life

St Magnus' Cathedral from the south-east

South doorway, St Magnus' Cathedral, showing the attractive use of different coloured flagstones

ST MAGNUS' CATHEDRAL

THIS IS A GOOD POINT at which to visit St Magnus' Cathedral, a twelfth-century triumph in red sandstone. It is relatively small compared with the huge cathedrals of the south such as Durham, York or Lincoln, but it possesses a unity of form which few other cathedrals can match. An excellent guide-book is available which explains the building's features in detail. The main points to look out for are these: first the stone, where the use of alternating and patterned blocks of red and ochre sandstone is one of the building's most striking features. Probably most of the stone came from the peninsula of Houlland, possibly some from Eday. Unfortunately all of it is rather soft so that a lot of patching has had to be done, not always with much sensitivity.

A first examination shows that the style is predominantly Romanesque, also that the building took a long time to complete, roughly three-and-a-half centuries. Its traditional foundation date is 1137. Like most ancient cathedrals, St Magnus' has suffered many vicissitudes, including virtual abandonment over long periods and threats of demolition on two occasions. Its present splendid condition is the result of an early twentieth-century restoration paid for by a group of public-spirited Orkney citizens led by Sheriff George Hunter McThomas Thoms. Sheriff Thoms is commemorated by the stained glass of the fine east window.

The interior is uncluttered, a place for worship rather than a gallery of memorials. There are, however, several notable monuments, including a small tablet which commemorates the six hundred men who drowned on HMS *Royal Oak* in Scapa Flow in 1940. Also remarkable are the monuments to two Orcadian-born Edinburgh doctors: one was William Balfour Baikie, a West African explorer who also translated parts of the Bible and prayer-book into Hausa. The other was John Rae, an Arctic explorer who, among his many achievements, surveyed the route of the undersea telegraph from Europe to North America via the Faroe islands and the overland telegraph from Winnipeg to the Pacific.

In 1968, the five hundredth anniversary of Orkney's union with Scotland, three more impressionistic representations of the cathedral's founders were added; they represent Kol the initiator, Rognvald the builder and Bishop William 'The Old', Kirkwall's first bishop.

MAGNUS THE SAINT

St Magnus' Cathedral has a unique history. First, though, who was St Magnus and what did he do?

Magnus was a most unusual Norse nobleman. He was killed 'for good reasons of state' because he tried to put into practice the peaceful and forgiving principles of Christianity in a century when the population seemed devoted to rivalry and bloodshed, even though it was sometimes prepared to attend church. His story is told in the *Orkneyinga Saga*.

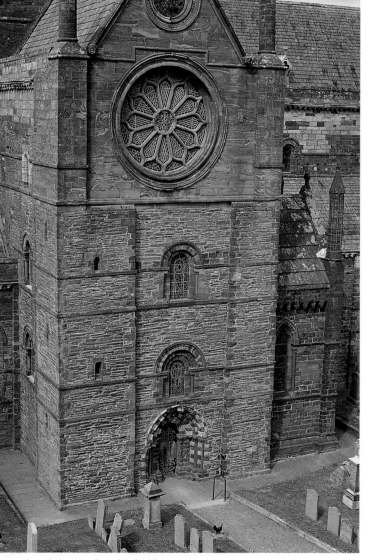

The south transept of St Magnus' Cathedral, seen from the Bishops' Palace

Magnus lived in the eleventh century when the earldom was divided between two brothers, Paul and Erlend; Magnus was Earl Erlend's eldest son. In 1098 the King of Norway, also named Magnus, arrived suddenly in Orkney to assert his authority. He unseated both the earls and shipped them back to Norway, appointed deputies in their place and then set off on a raiding expedition to Wales, taking Magnus Erlend's son with him.

25

SAGA DATES

Most dates suggested for events in the Orkneyinga Saga *are approximate. The declaimers of heroic stories in Norse drinking-halls were never much concerned about the precise years, months and days of the events they described. The date of the foundation of St Magnus' Cathedral, thought to be 1137, is perhaps fairly certain; but that of Earl Magnus' martyrdom is less so. Various authorities have calculated that it took place in 1115, 1116 or 1117. On balance, the latter date seems the most probable and it has been adopted in this book, subject to better information.*

Young Magnus made difficulties from the start: thus when the Norsemen decided to attack the Welsh rulers of Anglesey, he refused to take part and instead insisted on remaining on the royal ship and singing psalms. This overtly Christian behaviour greatly displeased King Magnus, and the earl's son had to disappear for several years until the king was dead. Probably he went to live at the Scottish court; we do not know.

By the time young Magnus reappeared, his father and uncle were also dead; Magnus therefore inherited half the Orkney earldom and his cousin Hakon, Paul's son, inherited the other half. Unhappily the two earls' followers soon fell out and a state approaching civil war developed. To resolve matters, it was decided that the two earls, each with a specified number of followers, should meet on the island of Egilsay to settle their differences; the time was round about Easter in the year 1117. Magnus and his escort landed first; but when Hakon appeared, he had a large force with him and clearly intended to remove his cousin from power once and for all. Moreover, some of his followers were determined that Magnus should be killed so that his followers should have no focus for their dissent.

None of Hakon's leading supporters was prepared to do the deed, however; and so eventually Hakon's cook, one Litolf, was deputed to strike the fatal blow. The *Saga* tells how Litolf sobbed and pleaded to be excused; but Magnus submitted to him with the words 'Be not afraid, for you do this against your will and he who forces you sins more than you do'. So Litolf struck off Magnus' head and in so doing created Orkney's first Christian martyr. The date is said to have been 16 April; and when Magnus was canonised, this was decreed as his commemoration day.

Magnus was buried in St Peter's church on the small islet of Birsay, the seat of Orkney's first bishops. Many years afterwards, when St Magnus' Cathedral was being built, his remains were transferred there, where they remain to this day. Is this a true story? Probably it is. In 1917, during the cathedral restoration, a cavity was discovered in the large rectangular pier of the choir's south arcade: inside was a box containing a broken skull and bones. In 1925 Dr R. W. Reid of Aberdeen University examined the remains and cautiously concluded that they matched the account of Magnus' death contained in the *Saga*. Whose bones could they be otherwise?

THE CATHEDRAL'S BUILDERS

The *Orkneyinga Saga* also tells us how the cathedral came to be built; it is a story of mixed motives. The initiative was taken by Orkney's most cultured and widely-travelled earl, named Rognvald but born as Kali; his father was Kol, nephew to St Magnus. Kali was brought up in Norway and developed pretensions to the Orkney earldom at an early age; but how to attain it? Earl Paul ruled securely in the islands, though the Norwegian king seemingly regarded him with increasing disfavour. Perhaps Paul appeared *too* secure, too independent.

At all events, in 1129 the king granted the earldom to Kali but left him to gain it; he was also required to change his name to Rognvald. Kali-now-Rognvald raised an expedition and set sail, only to meet with shipwreck and a repulse from Paul. Rognvald's father Kol then suggested a better plan: first, Rognvald was to announce that, when he secured the earldom, he would build the finest church in the north in memory of his saintly great-uncle; second, Earl Paul was to be kidnapped and spirited out of Orkney. This was done without delay; Paul was later murdered in Caithness. So Rognvald became Earl of Orkney and perhaps the most distinguished of them all. The *Saga* describes the colourful events of his life, including his voyage to the Holy Land; and it tells of how he honoured his pledge to build a splendid church in Kirkwall.

It is believed building began in 1137. Rognvald's father Kol supervised the great work and Rognvald himself came regularly to inspect progress. Soon, however, there was a shortage of money, but again the ingenious Kol hit upon a plan to solve it; he pointed out that Orkney's ødallers (yeomen farmers) had been deprived of their traditional rights of tenure by a previous earl, and suggested that Rognvald could restore these rights in return for cash payments. This was done, and construction of the cathedral continued. However, before the cathedral was anywhere near completed Rognvald was murdered by a rebellious chieftain in Caithness. Eventually his bones were returned to Kirkwall and placed in the cathedral he had founded, though their exact location was not known. Then in the eighteenth century the bones were re-discovered, set into the choir pillar opposite to that in which St Magnus' remains were found in the present century.

Slowly the cathedral took shape. Forty years after Rognvald's death the choir had been advanced to include three bays east from the crossing and an apse (since removed), while the six eastern bays of the nave had been completed. Subsequent extensions were slow and some modifications were made to the original plan. At one time the original tower collapsed. The final form of the cathedral as we see it today dates mainly from the thirteenth and fourteenth centuries, though all the interior fittings and glass are of course modern.

Visitors are usually surprised to learn that St Magnus' belongs to the town of Kirkwall and not to the Church of Scotland. This is because the cathedral was founded and built as an earldom property; it literally belonged to Earl Rognvald and his heirs and it still does. When in 1468 the King of Denmark transferred his personal tenure of the earldom to King James III of Scotland the cathedral went with the title and became King James' property. James, however, had no means of looking after the cathedral and it brought him no income, so he therefore transferred it to the 'Magistrates, Council and Community of Kirkwall', as a heritable possession and charged them with responsibility for its maintenance. This is the situation today. The Kirk of Scotland, which is not a cathedral body, uses St Magnus' as a parish church and so there have been no bishops in Orkney since 1688.

A CIVIL CATHEDRAL

St Magnus' Cathedral is unique in that it belongs to the City and Burgh Royal of Kirkwall. It is not and has never been a church property.

Twice in modern times, this municipal ownership has been contested, by the Crown in 1850–1 and by the Kirk of Scotland in 1925–9. Both challenges failed; but they served to establish once and for all the legal basis of the Burgh's ownership, thus set down in the New Statistical Account of 1842: 'The cathedral is the property of the provost, baillies, council and inhabitants of the burgh to whom it was gifted by the charter of James III, confirmed by a new charter from James V dated 1536, and a third by Charles II in 1661, ratifying the former two. Upon this charter infeftment [endowment as a heritable property] followed in 1669, and all these were confirmed by Act of Parliament, 1670, cap. 42.'

St Magnus' is literally Kirkwall's *cathedral.*

HIGH LIVING IN THE EARL'S PALACE

Earl Patrick lived in his palace in splendid style. The Historie and Life of King James the Sext *says of him that 'his pomp was so great, as he never went from his castle to the kirk, nor abroad otherwise, without the convoy of fifty muskateers, and other gentlemen of convoy and guard. And sichlike before dinner and supper, there were three trumpeters that sounded still till the meat of the first service was set at table, and sichlike at the second service, and, consequently, after the grace. He also had his ships directed to sea to intercept pirates and collect tribute of foreign fishers that came yearly to these seas. Whereby he made sic collection of great guns and other weapons for war, as no house, palace, nor castle, yea all in Scotland were not furnished with the like.'*

SPIRITUAL AND TEMPORAL POWERS: TWO PALACES

OPPOSITE ST MAGNUS' and a little way uphill stand two ruined palaces, once the residences and strongholds of bishops and of Orkney's last earls. The older of the two buildings is entered from the street called Watergate and was built for Orkney's bishops at around the time the cathedral was founded. It has been reconstructed and also badly damaged several times since. Today only the hall of a much larger structure survives, but the building is redolent with Orcadian history and is well worth an inspection. Here is a brief synopsis of the palace's historical origin:

Before St Magnus' was built, Orkney's bishops were based on the tidal islet of Birsay, also headquarters for Orkney's earls. When Rognvald seized the earldom, the Bishop of Orkney was one William, known as 'The Old' (1102–68). He became a crusading companion of Rognvald's and was a man of great learning and energy. He was a powerful support to Rognvald and his father in their cathedral-building enterprise and transferred the bishopric to Kirkwall as soon as St Magnus' was usable; almost certainly it was William who had the Bishops' Palace built.

Originally the palace had two storeys; and one point of interest is that the last King of Norway to visit Orkney died in its upper chamber in the winter of 1263, having been defeated mainly by storms and to a certain extent by Scotsmen in the confused 'battle' of Largs.

A RENAISSANCE GEM

OPPOSITE THE BISHOPS' PALACE stands the shell of one of Scotland's most elegant Renaissance buildings – it is also a memorial to the darkest and most oppressive period in Orkney's history. This is the sixteenth-century palace built by Earl Patrick Stewart, the last Earl of Orkney; he is said to have used slave labour, but could slave labour have built as well as this?

The last two Earls of Orkney had Scottish royal connections, as Robert the father of Patrick was an illegitimate son of James V. Both he and Patrick seem to have been extortioners and tyrants of the most extraordinary ferocity; even their contemporaries looked askance at their depredations. And yet they had many supporters in Orkney, and when the time came to fight off the king's armies, many men were ready to die for them. Therefore one feels that the full story of the Stewart earls has yet to be discovered.

Patrick Stewart built himself this palace immediately after his accession to the earldom in 1593; he is said to have forced his Orcadian subjects to quarry and ship in the stone and to do the building work without pay. He annexed the Bishops' Palace and incorporated it into one grandiose design. Castle building was a Stewart obsession: Patrick's father Robert built himself a large palace in Birsay, which his son improved, and Patrick also made additions to the splendid Noltland Castle in Westray, namely putting in an elegant stairway. Furthermore visitors to Shetland will see the fine towerhouse he built to overlook the harbour at Scalloway; and also Muness Castle in Unst, built by one of his client chiefs. However, as a consequence of all this castle building, Patrick Stewart incurred mountainous debts, and these caused him to intensify his exactions.

Relief for Orkney's people came at last through the intervention of another notable bishop, James Law (c1560–1632). Law informed James VI of the two earl's depredations and probably warned him of the danger posed by independent earls in islands which were at least as much Norse as Scottish, undoubtedly the more powerful argument. The king decided to bring the earls to heel, but how to do it? Kings of Scotland had no money to pay for expensive military expeditions in far-off islands. Then Earl George Sinclair of Caithness, who had personal scores to settle with the Stewarts, volunteered to lead and pay for an expedition himself – though its costs almost defeated him. However, after an armed rebellion by Patrick's son and a long and ineffectual bombardment first of the Bishops' Palace and then of the castle, both son and earl were eventually brought to Edinburgh for trial and execution. Earl George threatened to demolish St Magnus' Cathedral as a reprisal against the Orcadians, but fortunately Bishop Law persuaded him otherwise. So the Orkney earldom ended, and with it a most colourful period of Orkney's history.

The palace is now a two-storey building consisting of two long ranges built at right-angles one to another, a well-planned headquarters for a military household. There are huge cellars for the garrison stores, a large kitchen which was enlarged even while it was under construction, and a capacious well. Upstairs are an ante-room and

The Earl's Palace, a Renaissance architectural gem but a reminder of tyranny and the violent end of the earldom

audience chamber, the former equipped with washing facilities and a nobly proportioned great hall. The whole impression indicates excellent taste, a civilised and generous style of life, and absolute self-confidence; also a level of expenditure far beyond the means of rulers in these remote islands. Not surprisingly the building was left unfinished. An excellent guide-book is available to both palaces.

The architect and the chief mason for the Stewart palaces and strongholds were both Scotsmen, namely Andrew Crawford and John Ross. Both lie buried at Tingwall in Shetland.

ARTS, CRAFTS AND MANUFACTURERS

Orkney Islands Shipping Company ferries Varagen *and* Earl Sigurd *link Kirkwall with the north isles of Westray and Sanday*

KIRKWALL is packed with interest. For example, a visit to the Arts Theatre complex should not be missed: since the 1960s this centre has been developed as a major cultural asset, a place where international conferences are held and where music of the highest standard is performed. The development of music in Orkney owes much to the efforts of Sir Peter Maxwell Davies, who has a home in Hoy and whose compositions have often been inspired by Orkney's wild seas and landscapes, and also by the stirring events of its history, especially the story of St Magnus.

Orkney is farming country, and the best place to find out about farming is at the annual Orkney Show held in Bignold Park on the second Saturday of August; every aspect of Orcadian life is represented here. Visits may also be made to the world's most northerly whisky distillery, Highland Park; this produces a celebrated single malt and has a profitable export trade. There is a second distillery at Scapa. Those interested in the dairy industry and cheese-making in particular may wish to see the factory where the yellow and red Orkney cheeses are made. Orkney fudge is another local food product, exported all over Britain.

High-quality crafts are also well represented. For example, Ortak jewellery is designed and made in Kirkwall using symbols derived from the islands' archaeology; in 1993 Ortak was chosen to supply the new gift shop at Buckingham Palace, a notable distinction. Kirkwall is also the centre of a high-quality knitwear industry.

A link with the past. The coal-fired Earl Sigurd *which served the north isles until 1968. By tradition, most ferry boats working between Orkney, Shetland and Scotland have been named after earls or saints*

UPPIES AND DOONIES

Reference has been made already to the mass ball-game (the Ba') played on Christmas Day and New Year's Day in Kirkwall. It is one of Orkney's most remarkable events and probably dates back to Saga times; certainly a game of this kind is described in Gisli's Saga. There are in fact four Ba's these days: Boys' Ba's in the morning, and Mens' Ba's in the afternoon of each day.

The teams are made up from those who live south of the cathedral and palaces in the one-time earls' and bishops' town and who therefore play 'down-the gates' ('Doonies'); and those who live in the tradesmen's and fisher-men's town between cathedral and harbour and who play 'up-the-gates' ('Uppies'). 'Gate' derives from the Norse word for street, as it does in all areas of Norse or Danish settlement.

The Ba', one for each game, is donated by a notable supporter, often a former champion player, and is specially made of stitched leather for the occasion. The object of the game is to carry the Ba' either to the head of the town street at Mackinnon's Corner or to the harbour. Typically the Mens' Ba' starts at one o'clock and rages for up to six hours – there are exciting smuggles into the passages leading off the main street, sudden surges and forays and seemingly inextricable blockages. The scene is one of seething humanity, steam-ing in the chilly air. When the Ba' is carried to the harbour, a Doonie win, it is customary for a leading player to jump with it into the basin, an icy triumph. An Uppie win involves marginally less discomfort.

Immediately east of the harbour, Young Street leads through a small area known as Dunkirk where whale blubber used to be boiled down to produce oil for lamps or 'cruses' and other purposes. Beyond this area is the site of a Cromwellian fort, now marked only by a Territorial Army camp. Such forts were built in the north to protect shipping from Dutch and other privateers in the Commonwealth times.

There are still a few reminders of the two world wars in the town. The industrial estate at Hatston beside the coast road to Stromness began life as a Royal Naval Air Service (RNAS) station in the 1914–18 war. Some of its roads are named after World War II aircraft. Perhaps the most evocative relic of the second war is the Phoenix Cinema on Junction Road; it was always a refuge for serviceman and women on wet evenings and weekends and was customarily packed to the doors, however old the film happened to be.

Visitors who would like to make a more intensive study of Kirkwall are recommended to consult the Orkney Room at the library in Laing Street. One book is especially interesting: B. H. Hossack's *Kirkwall in the Orkneys*, published here in 1900; it is extremely readable and entertaining, and provides a 'pedigree' for every property in central Kirkwall up to that time.

Next we will move out from Kirkwall into West Mainland and begin to look at Orkney's archaeology and countryside. Both are in many respects unique: there is nowhere quite like Orkney.

3 THE FIRST ORCADIANS AND THEIR MONUMENTS

ANY LANDSCAPE BEARS THE IMPRINTS of prehistory and history and Orkney's landscapes look different from all others because the past of its various islands has been unique. A foray into West Mainland gives a very good introduction to the special character of this Orcadian landscape and to the long sequence of human occupation which is represented in it.

Leave Kirkwall across the Ayre or by the inland road past Wideford Hill and you come to nineteenth-century Finstown, one of Orkney's few true villages. It was home to Lord Grimond and his wife Laura, for more than forty years outstanding figures in local and national public life. 'Jo' Grimond was MP for Orkney and Shetland from 1950 to 1983 and was chief architect of the post-war Liberal Party.

West of Finstown there is a gap in low hills where a fine nineteenth-century estate house stands, Binscarth, from time to time home to various Lord Lieutenants of Orkney. Beyond the gap, the central lowland of West Mainland opens out, Orkney's only major inland area; and then comes Maes Howe, the most complete and memorable of all Britain's Neolithic monuments. Tormiston Mill opposite offers refreshments, and a guide-book is available.

MAES HOWE

MAES HOWE consists of a drystone burial cairn covered with turf and surrounded with a circular ditch; according to the best available calculations, building began around 2900–2800BC. The size of the cairn, the elaborate method of its construction, and its location near the centre of Orkney's largest land area all suggest that this was the burial place of a paramount family group which perhaps stood at the head of some kind of social hierarchy and was able to command labour from all the islands.

It is most unusual to be able to go inside a monument of this great age but Maes Howe is an exception. The entrance is through a long, low passage beneath enormous slabs of flagstone; inside there is a roomy chamber about four metres high, built up by overlapping pieces of stone and supported by

Left: the Ring of Brodgar

four huge vertical stone slabs at each corner. The domed roof is modern, the original having been dug out at the time of the first excavation in 1861. Two burial chambers open off the central space.

Maes Howe was empty when excavated. There had been visitors in earlier times and any treasures which it may just possibly have contained had been removed, together with the mass of disarticulated human bones which

were doubtless placed there. The most recent pre-modern visitors were Norse, who broke into the howe on more than one occasion and carved their graffiti on the walls, leaving us the finest collection of runic inscriptions in Britain. The runes tell us that at least one group of Norse howe-breakers were 'Jerusalem-farers' or pilgrims to the Holy Land, perhaps with Earl Rognvald. Another set records that the runes were cut with a valued axe, once the property of Gauk Trandillsson, who is known from the Sagas to have lived 150 years earlier in Iceland. Near the runic inscriptions, and quite hard to see, is the small drawing known as the Maes Howe 'lion' or 'dragon'; it has been compared to similar drawings in the church at Urness in Norway.

The runes remind us of the immense antiquity of Maes Howe. Viking times seem remote to us; yet when these runes were carved, the howe was already four-fifths its present age. Prehistory was long, far longer than history.

Norse howe-breakers' graffiti on the walls of Maes Howe. The runic writing, carved with an axe brought from Iceland, tells us that some of the Norsemen had lately returned from a crusade to the Holy Land. A full translation is available at the site

There are two basic designs of Neolithic burial cairn in Orkney, with many intermediate examples. Maes Howe with its central chamber is one type; a little further along the road towards Stromness is a good example of the other, a passage-like cairn with burials at the side. This is Onston (or Unstan) cairn, standing on a small peninsular jutting out into the Loch of Harray.

ONSTON AND TWO OTHER CAIRNS

CAIRNS of the Onston type are rather like burial ships built of flagstone. Usually their entrances are at one end, though Onston's is halfway along one side. Inside is a long central burial chamber flanked by eight stone recesses and with a small Maes Howe-type cell opposite the entrance. One of the burial recesses is unusual in that its threshold slab has obviously been worn by many feet; perhaps it came from the house of the notable person interred there. The upper part of the structure has been replaced by a modern roof; there may once have been a second storey to the chamber, as at Taversoe Tuick in Rousay.

Again there are Norse runes, though less interesting than those at Maes Howe. However, earlier visitors do not seem to have robbed the tomb and when excavated in 1884, it contained many disarticulated human remains, some fine flint implements, and the largest collection of Neolithic pottery ever found in Scotland. From the multitude of fragments it was possible to reconstruct more than half of six broad, shallow bowls, decorated under their rims. These vessels are to be seen in Edinburgh's Museum of Antiquities, and have given their name to Onston ware; they are regarded as important markers in the evolution of prehistoric pottery in Europe.

Onston is much older than Maes Howe – it was probably in active use for burials by 3400BC.

Two other less elaborate Neolithic burial cairns may be inspected in West Mainland. The circular Wideford Hill cairn stands on the slopes of Wideford Hill just above the 'old' or inland road from Kirkwall to Finstown. It was excavated in 1849 but found to have been ransacked in earlier ages. It is circular in form.

Curween Hill cairn south of Finstown is more elaborate. It consists of an oblong central chamber with four side-cells and its entrance is through a long, low passage. Curween was excavated in 1901, and although there had been the usual earlier visitors, the contents were relatively undisturbed: there were some human remains, and also the bones of an ox, a horse and more than two dozen dogs (or were they foxes?). Possibly dogs were kept to strip the flesh from corpses exposed before interment. Birds, including eagles, served the same purpose.

Keys to these monuments are held nearby; the Orkney Tourist Board will advise about access. A powerful torch is needed in order to see anything.

HISTORY OF THE ORKNEY CAIRNS
AND THEIR BUILDERS

THERE ARE seventy-six known chambered cairns in Orkney. They appear to have been built as communal burial places for extended family groups, constructed where they could be seen by the communities they served and used for many centuries. In theory, if an undisturbed example could be found, it might be possible to work out how many people lived around it at any one time; assuming of course that the earliest and latest bones could be dated and that all members of the community were interred in it. Some progress has in fact been made with investigations along these lines, notably by Professor Colin Renfrew at Quanterness cairn west of Kirkwall.

REFLECTIONS ON THE STONES

'At Stennis, in the Mainland, where the Loch is narrowest, in the middle, having a Causey of Stones over it for a Bridge, there is, at the South-end of the Bridge, a Round, set about with high smooth Stones or Flags, about twenty Foot high above ground . . . Betwixt that Round and the Bridge are two Stones standing of that same largeness with the rest . . . and at both East and West of this Bigger Round, are two artificial (as it is thought) green mounts.

'Some think that these Rounds have been places whereon two opposite Armies have encamped; but I think it more probable that they have been the high places of Pagan *times, whereon Sacrifice was offered, and that these two Mounts were the places where the Ashes of the Sacrifice were flung . . .'*

Dr James Wallace, FRS, 1700

More than 12,500 human bone fragments were found in this large cairn. By meticulous sorting it was possible to show that these came from 157 individuals who had been interred over a period of about five-and-a-half centuries. The age and sex compositions of the interments could be deduced, suggesting that all members of the community were buried in the cairn, though there must always be some doubt on this point.

The Quanterness studies suggest that about 15–20 people lived here at any one time in the Neolithic. Their life expectancy was a mere 20–25 years and physically they were very like ourselves. By using these figures as a base, it is then possible to estimate the total population of Neolithic Orkney as between 2,000 and 6,000 people. On balance the higher figure seems the more probable, bearing in mind the amount of building that was done.

THE HENGE MONUMENTS STENNESS AND BRODGAR

FURTHER EVIDENCE of the focal importance of central West Mainland in Neolithic times is to be found in the two henge monuments of Stenness and Brodgar, both close to Maes Howe. These two striking monuments dominate the narrow neck of land which separates the salty waters of the Loch of Stenness from the freshwater Loch of Harray. Four very large stones survive at Stenness, while the Brodgar circle has twenty-seven standing and nine fallen stones – in fact Brodgar once consisted of sixty monoliths. Local farmers through the centuries have carted the missing stones away for gateposts and to help build their houses and barns. A deep circular ditch surrounds the Brodgar circle, and the earth from this was originally used to build a high bank enclosing the whole monument; in Neolithic times it would have looked like an enclosure of upright stones, partly hidden from view by its surrounding earthwork. However, the bank seems to have been used by local farmers as a handy source of good soil to add to their fields, and no visible signs of it remain.

Both henges date from around 3000BC and would appear to mark the central site of long-forgotten religious and social ceremonies. Possibly the ceremonies were associated with the paramount family in Orkney whose members were interred in Maes Howe. Certainly an enormous amount of work by a large number of people, skilfully managed, was needed to raise the stones and build the howe; one recent calculation puts the number of standard man-hours needed to erect Stenness and Brodgar at between 85,000 and 200,000. Looking at the giant stones one is inclined to favour the higher figure.

What were the henge monuments for? We do not know for certain; but Professor Eric Thom has proposed an ingenious theory which suggests that they were astronomical observatories, used to predict eclipses and to

make other astronomical and astrological calculations. The theory is based upon a detailed study of all Britain's henge monuments and does appear plausible. Certainly Brodgar stands at the centre of a vast circle of open sky, an ideal situation for an astronomical observatory. If it had other purposes, what could they have been?

The Ring of Brodgar, a splendid henge monument in the centre of West Mainland. This is William Daniell's view, drawn in 1818

RECENT FINDS IN SOUTH RONALDSAY

AT THE SOUTH END of South Ronaldsay near the Burwick ferry terminal, are the recently excavated Neolithic sites at Isbister farm. The most important remains are those of a chambered cairn and a 'burnt mound', of which a large number are marked, somewhat mysteriously, on maps of Orkney.

Over page: the Ring of Brodgar, a stone circle set beneath open skies. Was it a pre-historic obsvervatory?

When the chambered cairn was first investigated during the 1980s it was found not to have been disturbed. Examination of its contents – which included the remains of more than three hundred individuals – dating from around 3100BC to about 1600BC, together with evidence leading to knowledge of the food the people ate and the tools they used, has added fresh details to our comprehension of Orkney's prehistory. It has been possible to reconstruct age-pyramids for the Isbister community in Neolithic times, to establish that their average life expectancy was perhaps around thirty years, and that they were similar in stature to ourselves, also muscular because of hard physical work but subject to the diseases associated with cold and damp conditions such as arthritis. They grew wheat as well as the ancient variety of barley called *bere,* herded cattle and sheep, gathered birds' eggs and fished the local sea.

Skara Brae, one of several Neolithic hut clusters found in Orkney, and the island's most-visited archaeological site

Near to the chambered cairn are the excavated remains of a 'burnt mound'. These mounds are associated with enormous amounts of burned pottery fragments, ash and carbon deposits, and their purpose has long been a matter of debate. Evidence from this example, undisturbed until it was excavated, suggests that it was simply a rubbish tip, placed beside a building used perhaps to boil whole animal carcasses on hot stones. This method is known from Ireland and the Hebrides, and its practicability was demonstrated on a BBC *Chronicle* programme. Alternatively it may have been a communal warm bath. Not all 'burnt mounds' necessarily had the same function, however: visitors to Isbister may like to read the guide-book and make up their own minds about the fascinating evidence, insofar as this is possible.

SKARA BRAE NEOLITHIC VILLAGE

WHERE DID THE BUILDERS of the Neolithic burial cairns and henge monuments live? Few domestic structures of this great age survive anywhere in Europe, but on the Bay of Skaill in West Mainland there is a spectacular exception: Skara Brae, Orkney's most-visited archaeological site. It consists of a group of 'Stone-Age' huts built from unmortared stone, linked together by passages. Its survival into modern times is the fortunate result of quick burial by advancing sand-dunes which 'mothballed' it for about forty centuries; and of exposure just at the time when archaeology was becoming a science and there were informed people living in Orkney who understood the significance of what was being brought to light. Without this combination of circumstances, Skara Brae might have vanished without trace.

The story of Skara Brae's discovery is remarkable. In about 1850, storms began to move the Skaill Bay sand-dunes inland, which uncovered previously buried stone structures. Amateur investigators examined the structures from time to time between 1855 and 1913 and most concluded that they were medieval. This view was supported by the supposed discovery of a stone inscribed with a Christian cross, although subsequently it transpired that the stone had not come from this site at all. Then from 1927 onwards, Professor Gordon Childe, one of the most distinguished archaeologists of his day, made a full scientific study of the site on behalf of the then Office of Works. His findings revealed that Skara Brae was Neolithic, not medieval, an astounding discovery because of the rarity of such sites anywhere in Europe at anything like this state of preservation.

There is no doubt about Skara Brae's great age. Professor Childe and those who have studied the site more recently have found absolutely no traces of metal. The people who lived here for more than six centuries used tools made

Detail of one of the excavated family huts at Skara Brae, showing flagstone box-beds and other furnishings. In the background is Skaill House, since Norse times one of Orkney's most important properties

from bone and flint. They herded cattle and sheep, but had great difficulty in sustaining their animals through the winter; they used horses for hunting red deer and wild boar, numerous remains of which were found around the site. They gathered shellfish in large quantities but did no other fishing; and they may have been cultivators, but this is uncertain – though many of Orkney's Neolithic peoples certainly were. In particular they grew the early ripening variety of barley called *bere*, a few fields of which are grown today in the islands and Caithness. Bere may be recognised by its yellow colour in summer, whereas modern barley will still be green and not ready for harvest until mid-August at the earliest.

THE SKARA BRAE SITE

The excavated and preserved site consists of eight inter-connecting huts, roofless but in a very good state of repair; each is roughly rectangular in plan. Low, covered passages run between the huts, now partly open to the sky; access to each hut is through a low doorway from the passage outside.

The huts contain a remarkable array of flagstone furniture: modern-looking cupboards and a 'dresser', bed spaces and small fish-tanks on the floor which are thought to have been used to keep shellfish fresh. Each hut has a central hearth.

There are hints that this society was hierarchical. Hut One, nearest the shore is larger than the others and probably belonged to the community's leading family; while the bed space to the right of each hut doorway is always the largest, probably because it was used by the head of the household. This arrangement is reminiscent of sleeping arrangements in Orkney houses down to modern times, and also of Black Houses in the Hebrides. Guanche dwellings in the Canary Islands follow a similar plan.

Before it was excavated and cleaned up, Skara Brae was entombed in a mountain of shells and other human debris. The cocooning was deliberate: it helped to insulate the huts and passage-ways from the weather and hid them from possible enemies. Life in the subterranean huts was undoubtedly smoky, smelly and dark, and not at all to modern taste; but probably it was relatively comfortable by the standards of the time.

Skara Brae was not built on the shore – such a site would have been unnecessarily exposed. In fact the Atlantic waves have been encroaching here from time immemorial; and the rate of erosion in recent times can be gauged from the evidence of Skaill Mill, recently demolished, a short distance north of Skara Brae. This was built in 1700 about 50 metres from the coast, but since the 1960s the sea had been undermining it. Given this rate of marine advance, we may assume that the Skara Brae community lived well inland, behind a sheltering line of dunes. Exactly how far is impossible to calculate because of the ever-changing outline of the coast.

How old is Skara Brae? This is a simple question, but very difficult to answer. It is, of course, impossible to date a stone-built structure by carrying

Skara Brae: a passage connecting the huts, originally buried under a great pile of midden for warmth and protection

out any chemical or other kind of test on the stones themselves, and so dating has to be attempted by using human and animal remains and artefacts associated with the structures. In Orkney this task has been made doubly difficult because of the   activities of howe-breakers in ancient times and amateur archaeologists more recently: both have removed important evidence. One hopes that modern archaeologists are not doing the same, despite their improved techniques.

Nevertheless, it is possible to say that people began to live in the Skara Brae huts as early as 3200BC and that they continued to do so for between six and ten centuries. Towards the end of this period there was first a temporary evacuation, then a final one, by which time the advancing sand-dunes must have become overwhelming. An excellent official guide-book and photographs are available at the site which is in the care of Historic Scotland.

THE BROCHS, A MYSTERY

THE ROMAN OCCUPATION of Britain does not appear to have affected Orkney at all. After a preliminary reconnaissance of the north in the first century AD during which, according to Tacitus, Orkney was 'taken' and Shetland seen in the distance, the Roman authorities decided that neither profit nor threat were to be expected from this remote quarter. They therefore withdrew to the fertile and productive parts of the country south of the Moray Firth, and as far as we know never ventured so far north again.

During the centuries of Roman rule, however, certain as yet unexplained changes took place in Orkney's political circumstances which have left their mark on the landscape in the shape of an enormous number of fortified stone towers, called brochs. It looks as though just about every community in Orkney and more in Shetland, Caithness and along the West Highland coast of Scotland decided to build themselves refuges into which they could retreat when attacked – although there is no indication of who the attackers were. The building effort must have been staggering and was probably unnecessary; the Orkney towers never seem to have been used for defence. Soon after they were built, domestic structures were added both inside and out, making them indefensible.

Altogether 106 broch sites are known in Orkney; and there are another 95 in Shetland, and 239 on the Scottish north and west coasts. Several of the

The Broch of Borwick, sited on a precipitous headland on the West Mainland coast

Orcadian examples are well-preserved, but to see an intact broch it is necessary to visit the tiny isle of Mousa off the east coast of Shetland.

A good example to visit in West Mainland is the Broch of Borwick, which stands at the edge of a precipitous cliff some two kilometres south of the bay of Skaill; it may be reached by a spectacular cliff-top scramble from north or south. About half the tower survives, with a low entrance which is fairly complete. Crawling through this passage one passes a stone-built 'guard house', a typical broch feature. On the coastal side the broch wall has fallen down the cliff, evidence of continuing coastal erosion. Inside the broch, a confused scattering of stones probably indicates the remains of later domestic structures; according to the standard pattern of broch construction, there should be a well under these stones. Outside the broch, bumps in the grass show where there was formerly a whole complex of domestic structures, built to a radial or 'wheelhouse' pattern.

The Broch of Gurness, an enormous example of an Iron Age fortified tower, engulfed in later domestic buildings, some of them Norse

A much larger and more complicated example is the Broch of Gurness on the east coast of Mainland, northwest of Kirkwall. This site is open to the public, and there is a museum and a guide-book. Like Borwick, Gurness occupies a peninsular site, difficult of access; there is a beach nearby where boats would have been drawn up, and the view is extensive, suggesting that the expected attackers would have come by sea.

Gurness is huge; it is also excessively complicated in layout. In essence it consists of the original broch, a massive structure dating from the first century AD; and an untidy collection of later domestic buildings inside and outside the tower, including some which were built on top of an infilled defensive ditch. To add to the complication, several Norse-age longhouses were added later. It is impossible to tell whether these Norse incomers built their houses next to a friendly First Orcadian community or whether the broch and its domestic dwellings had been abandoned before the Norse families arrived.

Another mighty broch, Midhowe, stands in full view on the Rousay shore opposite Gurness. This will be described in a section dealing with that island. First, however, we will look at two other notable sites in Mainland located at the extreme north-east and north-west extremities of the island, namely the Brough of Deerness and the Brough of Birsay. The sites record the coming of Christianity to Orkney, first in the pre-Norse or Pictish period, then in the early Norse period itself.

4 CHRISTIAN BEGINNINGS

DEERNESS AND ITS CHAPEL

NEAR THE NORTH-EASTERN tip of Mainland stands a small, rocky islet of red sandstone, and on top of this inaccessible and bleak extremity the remains of what may have been a Celtic or Pictish-age chapel can be seen. There are fine cliffs and bays hereabouts and many seabirds; but it is a wild and unprotected place on a rough day.

Little is known about the chapel, but it is just the kind of simple structure, located in a remote place, which the Celtic clergy favoured. That branch of the early church had no time for splendid cathedrals, elaborate ceremonies and ecclesiastical hierarchies; consequently it was unable to maintain its position against the centralised and highly organised power of the Roman church.

Access to the islet involves a rough scramble down to sea-level and a steep climb to the chapel site. Shoes with a good tread are necessary here. From the chapel there are fine views along the north coast of Mainland to Mull Head and across the sea to the low north isle of Sanday.

A little way south is a fine example of a geo, a trench-like, vertically-sided inlet cut into the cliffs by waves exploiting a line of weakness in the rocks. This chasm ends in a cave, the roof of which has partly collapsed to form a gloup or 'blow-hole'; in the depths below the sea may be heard surging in an alarming manner. This is a place to be approached with extreme care.

THE BROUGH OF BIRSAY

AT THE NORTH-WEST tip of Orkney Mainland, there is a small tidal islet, accessible on foot at low water only, on which may be seen a unique assemblage of ruins. Most are Norse but some date from the pre-Norse Pictish period. The islet is a massive tilted slab of sandstone with striking cliffs facing the Atlantic. The landward side of the great slab is grassy and sheltered and it has played a notable part in Orcadian history as a base for sea-earls and bishops, and possibly for a great Pictish family before them.

The complicated arrangement of ruins is best understood with the aid of an air photograph and guide-book, sometimes obtainable at the site. The

ORKNEY'S BURMA ROAD

Visitors who walk to the Brough of Deerness may be surprised to find what looks like a length of Roman road on the cliff-top. In fact, this is a relic of World War II, when thousands of soldiers were stationed on Orkney with little to do. This road was built laboriously by hand to keep them occupied; it seems to have had no other purpose.

It was known as the Burma Road after the other great road-building enterprise of the 1940s, the supply-road into China from the west.

Brough of Birsay: Earl Thorfinn's Great Christ Church or 'Peter Kirk', seat of Orkney's bishops before St Magnus' was built

most obvious remains date from the time of Earl Thorfinn, who came to power in 1020 and who made the Orkney earldom a force to be reckoned with in northern Scotland. Anyone who decides to dip into the *Orkneyinga Saga* might well begin with Thorfinn. It tells us of an able and energetic man, skilled in politics and with immense effrontery, an expert in sailing near the wind and favoured by good luck at certain critical times in his career; one feels, too, that he usually improved his luck by careful planning.

Although in theory his position was tributary to the Norwegian Crown, Thorfinn managed to build up his power without provoking a naval intervention from Norway. He extended his influence southwards into Scotland, where he engaged in successful military actions against King Duncan, that same Duncan who appears fleetingly in Shakespeare's *Macbeth*. Thorfinn lived the last seventeen years of his life on the islet of Birsay where he built himself a palace and a fine church nearby. Orkney's bishops were also based at this church until St Magnus' Cathedral was built in Kirkwall. Thorfinn died in 1064 and was buried in his Birsay church.

The Norse ruins on the brough include those of Earl Thorfinn's palace, a well-equipped building with under-floor central heating and a bath house; his Great Christ Church or Peter Kirk; a Viking-age boat slip; the remains of monastic buildings constructed on the site of the palace after this had burned down; and a number of Norse longhouses.

Underneath the complex of *Saga*-age structures it is just possible to make out some remains of Celtic buildings of uncertain purpose, though possibly ecclesiastical in part. A Pictish-age well and evidences of metal working have been revealed by excavation, but the most striking discovery has been that of a Pictish symbol-stone (a replica now stands on the site; the original is in Edinburgh). It is what is termed a Class 2 stone, but it is unique in that it depicts three warriors in addition to four of the standard Pictish symbols. It is believed that these three finely carved figures, ceremonially clothed and carrying swords as signs of their high office, represent members of a wealthy and powerful family based on the Brough of Birsay in Pictish times.

The significance of Pictish symbol-stones is hotly debated. Recently, Anthony Jackson has tabulated and classified the symbols on all the 233 known symbol-stones in Scotland and suggested that they record lineages and political alliances through marriage. Unfortunately the sample on which this explanation is based is rather small, and the discovery of some more stones with predicted sets of symbols is needed to confirm it.

The whole Pictish period which the Birsay stone and ruins represent lasted for many centuries and overlapped the period of Norse settlement. The Picts seem to have been a political organisa-

Replica of the Pictish symbol-stone found on the Brough of Birsay

tion of peoples already present in Scotland. All the evidence suggests they developed a high level of culture and artistic achievement, yet because they left no written records, we know little about them. The Pictish dominion certainly extended to Orkney; and it was in Pictish times that Christianity was brought here, centuries before the point-of-sword so-called conversion of the Norse Orcadians by King Olav Tryggvason in 995, as recorded in the *Saga*.

The parish of Birsay, inland from the brough, is often called the garden of Orkney because of its fertility. Here, Thorfinn seems to have settled his followers and their families in large numbers. Even today about forty families in the Birsay district can claim descent from Norse times, something which is unusual in the rest of Orkney because of disturbance in the Scots period.

THE EARL'S BU' IN ORPHIR

The Orkneyinga Saga *gives us a first-hand description of the Earl's Bu' in Orphir: 'There is at Orphir a large drinking-hall, and there was a door in the south wall under the east gable, and a magnificent church stood facing the hall door; and one went down steps from the hall to the church. And when one entered the hall there was on the left a large flagstone and (between it and the hall) were a number of large ale-casks; but opposite the outer door there was a small room.' (Alexander B. Taylor's translation.)*

The accuracy of this description has been confirmed by Mr A. W. Johnston's excavations in 1899–1901 and by more recent studies. The Saga *writer once stood in this hall!*

Much later, after the union with Scotland, one of Thorfinn's Scottish successors, Earl Robert Stewart, built himself another palace on Birsay mainland. Today its gaunt shell dominates the view southwards from the brough. This very large ruin has lately been renovated and is an interesting place to visit.

So we see in Birsay both the beginning and the end of the Orkney earldom: its beginning as a significant political force in the eleventh century with Earl Thorfinn, master of the northern seas; and its end, clouded with oppression and tyranny in the seventeenth century, with the Stewart earls. Earl Robert died in 1593, by which time the earldom had only twenty-two stormy years to run.

Also in Birsay and well worth visiting if it is open, is Boardhouse Mill, previously mentioned. It is the last working example of an estate mill, which formerly ground bere for local consumption and barley for export to the Highlands. It dates from 1873 and is now the property of Orkney Islands Council.

ORPHIR'S ROUND CHURCH

ANOTHER FRAGMENT of a church dating from Norse times is to be found in Orphir, the district of Mainland facing Hoy. This is the well-preserved apse of a unique round church, modelled upon the Church of the Holy Sepulchre in Jerusalem. Its plan suggests its origin. After the slaying of Magnus, Earl Hakon, secure in the earldom but troubled in his conscience, decided to make a pilgrimage to Jerusalem. On his return he built this small, elegant church as a memorial to his great journey.

Originally the round church consisted of a circular nave, of which only part of the east end survives; and an apse, which is surprisingly complete. The building dates from the late eleventh century and is built in local stone, mortared with a mixture rich in lime which gives the structure its light colouring. It survived almost complete until the mid-eighteenth century, but then much of its stone was used to build a much larger parish church, to which this fragment was attached. The larger church has now been cleared away.

The church is mentioned once in the *Orkneyinga Saga*; this also tells us that the earls' Bu' or drinking hall stood nearby, the foundations of which were discovered in 1859. The *Saga* recounts a number of violent incidents, and mentions a number of leading men associated with this drinking hall; many nursed their rivalries and some died savage deaths here. Some of the bloodiest drinking parties seem to have been punctuated by visits to the church nearby. There was no polite society in an earl's drinking hall.

Like Birsay, this was an early centre of power in Orkney before Kirkwall was finally established as capital in the time of Earl Rognvald, Kali's son. An interpretation centre, devoted to life in the Norse period, is to be developed here when funds allow.

Apse of the round church in Orphir, built by Earl Hakon, the slayer of Magnus, after his penitential journey to Jerusalem

Traditional Orkney longhouse with grain-drying kiln: Upper House, Harray

5 A TIMELESS COUNTRY

FROM ØDALLERS TO RIGHTLESS TENANTS

NORSE ORKNEY, which has left us Earl Thorfinn's palace and church, Earl Hakon's round church and Earl Rognvald's great cathedral in Kirkwall, gradually gave place to Scots Orkney, most strikingly represented by the Stewart earls' palaces. For most people, however, the change probably went almost unnoticed. In Kirkwall there may have been sieges and bombardments, but in the countryside change was slow indeed and it remained so for several centuries; thus a visitor in the early eighteenth century would have seen an Orkney little different from that of the thirteenth. So what was life in this seemingly timeless countryside like, and what reminders of those years exist in the country we see today?

For about sixty years Orkney has been a land of small owner-farmers and at the height of the *Saga* period seven centuries ago things were somewhat similar. Then, independent yeomen farmers called 'ødallers' held their lands from the earl, who in turn held all Orkney on behalf of the Norwegian Crown. But between these two widely separated times, Orkney was divided into large estates, mostly owned by Scottish lairds, and on these estates the people who worked the land were tenants without rights. All three of these very different phases of Orkney history are represented in the modern landscape.

First, what can we see now of the Norse period, apart from the obvious churches and archaeological remains? The answer lies in the settlement pattern. When the Norse colonists took over the lands of Orkney, probably eating the First Orcadian inhabitants out of house and home as they did so, they established a pattern of scattered farms which persists to this day. Dispersed settlement is characteristic of all the Scandinavian lands, and in Orkney it is particularly noticeable in the inland district of West Mainland, Stenness and Harray, where there always seems to be a house in view.

Naturally the Norse incomers chose the best land, the same land which had long been farmed by the First Orcadians. As a result, Norse Orkney must have looked very like Neolithic Orkney: there would have been patches of cultivated land dotted with houses, surrounded by rough grazings and then by heather moors. The moors yielded peat, which was the main source of fuel.

A loose grouping of farms was called a *tun*; the Scots took over this word and changed it to *toon*, later *township*, the term still used today. When

A PEAT MYSTERY

Peat has been Orkney's domestic fuel for many centuries – but not always. According to the Orkneyinga Saga, the earliest Norse settlers did not know about peat's valuable properties and had to be shown how to use it by Earl 'Turf' Einar in about the year 900.

Peat would have been unfamiliar to people from Norway's western fiords, but it was also of fairly recent origin in Orkney itself and the pre-Norse Orcadians may not have made much use of it. Peat formation took place in the centuries immediately prior to the Norse colonisation, probably for two main reasons: the climate became cool and wet, while the land was badly over-grazed by cattle raised for export. Bad weather and too many animals would have allowed the build-up of acid conditions in the degraded soils and so favoured the growth of peat-bogs.

ØDAL RIGHTS ENDURE

*'The Al-odh-ial or Odh-al holding
was the only tenure of land
recognised in Scandinavian
kingdoms. It was transmitted by
Odin's followers to their offspring,
as the dearest of those free
institutions which distinguished
them from servile races, willing to
hold their lands as the gift of a
master . . . the Ødal idea is the
negation of every Feudal principle.*

*The Odh-al-Raedi or Right of
Full Possession, was a tacit entail
upon the Primal Occupant and his
Heirs of the Ødalsjord won by his
strong right hand, complete
without a written title, subject to
no service . . . comprising every
conceivable right of use, ownership
and possession, and at his death,
constituting in each of his children
an equal, tacit title, inalienable
while one Ødal-born descendant
should exist to claim the
inheritance.'*

David Balfour of Balfour and
Trenaby. Ødal Rights and Feudal
Wrongs *(Edinburgh, 1860)*

parish organisation was introduced in Norse times, neighbouring *tuns* were assembled into parishes. Probably many parish boundaries followed much older divisions of the land. Similarly, many Norse farms were built on top of what had been Neolithic sites. It looks as though the leading Norse families appropriated the lands farmed by leading pre-Norse families, often indicated by the site of a broch. Continuity has always been a dominant theme in the Orcadian countryside.

The Norse settlers held their lands from the earl under ødal law, which gave them absolute security of tenure providing they did not displease the earl too seriously. In return they paid him a tax called *scat*, and the earl in turn paid a duty to the Crown. *Scat* survived into recent times as superior duty, payable to the Crown as legal inheritor of the Norse earldom.

Ødal properties customarily extended to low water-mark; consequently Orkney farmers may fence their land down to the edge of the sea, making coastal walks difficult. (Elsewhere in Britain, all foreshores belong to the Crown.) Ødal rights also extend below ground and in theory at least give the landowner rights to anything of value down to the centre of the earth. (Elsewhere in Britain all minerals are Crown property.) The provisions of ødal law can still be significant when possible cases of treasure trove arise; thus there have been some interesting legal battles over buried treasure in modern times in the former Norse earldom, notably that involving church treasure found on St Ninian's Isle in Shetland which was proven ødal land. Generally speaking, however, it can be difficult to prove beyond doubt that ødal rights have been maintained through the centuries over a given plot of land. The fact remains that no court has ever had the authority to abrogate ødal law, and lawyers keep well clear of ødal-related cases if they can.

Unhappily for the Orcadians, the independence conferred by ødal tenure did not last. This was mainly because of Norse inheritance arrangements which required properties to be divided between all sons and daughters. It took remarkably few generations to reduce many farms to sub-economic plots, and their tenants to economic and political impotence. This was the diminished Orkney society which the Scots eventually took over; and the further step of transforming impoverished smallholders into rightless tenants on estates was an easy and logical one to take.

After the union with Scotland most of the new estate owners were Scottish incomers. Some estate-owning families became reformers who brought modern ideas about farming and estate management across the Pentland Firth; others did nothing with their lands and as much for their tenants.

There followed a shadowy period in Orkney's history during which the countryside remained almost unchanged for the better part of three centuries. What is there to see today of that arrested countryside? Signs of it are fading fast, but there are some interesting reminders in the form of traditonal Orkney houses. A few of these survive in remote corners of the islands; in West Mainland, two have been turned into farm museums.

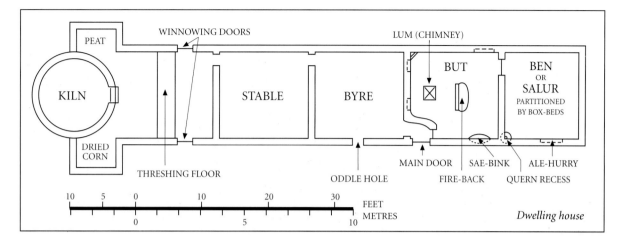

PEAT

WINNOWING DOORS

LUM (CHIMNEY)

BUT

BEN
OR
SALUR
PARTITIONED
BY BOX-BEDS

KILN

STABLE

BYRE

DRIED
CORN

THRESHING FLOOR

ODDLE HOLE

MAIN DOOR

SAE-BINK

ALE-HURRY

FIRE-BACK

QUERN RECESS

10 5 0   10   20   30   FEET
                              METRES
     0   5   10

Dwelling house

TRADITIONAL ORKNEY HOUSES

IN THE NORSE PERIOD and for centuries afterwards, Orkney's people lived mostly in longhouses, built with unmortared stone and roofed with thatch. One end of a longhouse was the family home, the other was kept for animals and grain storage. The old houses came in many sizes according to the relative prosperity of their occupants. The more elaborate versions might consist of two parallel buildings, the second consisting of a separate byre, stable, barn and threshing-space, with a kiln at the end to dry grain.

Kiln detail, Corrigall Farm Museum, before renovation

The kiln-ended longhouse was *the* characteristic Orkney house form. Unfortunately examples have lately become rare as surviving ruins are robbed for stone or cleared away.

Only one surviving longhouse dates with a fair degree of certainty to the time of the Norse earldom: this is Winksetter, a fine example on private land set below the hills of West Mainland. Two other striking longhouses have been preserved as farm museums at Corrigall and Kirbuster, both in central West Mainland; Corrigall is an especially fine restoration and is the more interesting of the two houses. Its site is very ancient, as is shown by the presence of an Iron Age broch nearby. Clearly a Neolithic community once farmed this land. The farmhouse is representative of the most elaborate kind of longhouse, and has a

Byre with flagstone cattle stalls,
Corrigall

byre and kiln-ended barn built behind it. There is also the shell of a smaller watermill built over a stream which once ground bere and oats for the local community.

Today it is hard to imagine what life might have been like in a house such as the one at Corrigall, as restoration has made it deceptively light, tidy and clean. When humans and animals shared a building without windows, the walls of which were plastered with a mixture of oat husks, clay and cow dung, and where a peat fire smouldered day and night, the reality must have been dark, smoky and smelly, even though warm.

Whatever their size, old Orkney houses had similar features: there was one entrance for both people and animals; and the family living space was always at the higher end of the house, divided by a wall into two sections called the *but* and the *ben*. The *but* was nearest the door and was an all-purpose space used as family sleeping area and kitchen and for animals needing special care – thus calves would be reared in the *but* and one might find a sow and her litter of piglets; hens would perch in the roof space overhead. The living part and the animal-tending part of the *but* were divided by the fire *back*, a massive block of stone where the household fire burned and which was the social focus for the family and visitors. Smoke escaped through a hole in the roof called a *lum*, a cowl-like construction made of boards. The *lum* was the only source of light in the house.

The *ben* was the windowless living space farthest from the door; here the farmer and his wife slept in a small degree of privacy.

Next to the *but* was the byre where at least one cow would be stalled, while the stable would accommodate at least one horse; sometimes cattle and horses were kept together. In winter, all the farmer's livestock had to be brought indoors to protect them from the cold and biting winds. This winter-stalling of farm animals continues today and accounts for the deserted fields which are a feature of the Orkney countryside in winter.

Inside the living quarters, furniture was rudimentary. Originally most of it was made of flagstone on the 'Skara Brae' model, but in the eighteenth and nineteenth centuries wooden furniture was generally substituted, although at Corrigall stone-fitted furniture was in use until the present century. The main items were beds, originally stone-built neuk beds set into the thickness of the walls but in more recent times box-beds made of wood and free-standing; also simple shelves, and cupboards and chairs, the latter very plain and hard. The fine high-backed Orkney chairs which are sold today as traditional items were in fact always a rarity, the preserve of the well-to-do. Stone-fitted furniture was in use until the present century, and Corrigall has good examples.

A flagstone shelf usually set into a corner of the house would be the quern alcove or *ledder* where grain was ground by hand, using a mortar-and-pestle. Incidentally grinding was always done 'with the sun', as were all household and farm tasks requiring any kind of circular motion – to work anti-clockwise was thought to invite bad luck. Another shelf in the *but* end would be the *sae-bink*, holding a jar of fresh water. In the *ben* end, under the personal supervision of the head of the household, was the ale-*hurry* or shelf where beer was kept. A cupboard-like space at floor level might be reserved for a goose.

Thick walls, a gun-loop window, spaces in the walls for hens and a goose, all common features of traditional Orkney longhouses

In poorer houses the floor was of beaten earth; the better-off, as at Corrigall, would flag their floors. The roof was of thatch, supported on a frame of driftwood or imported timbers; the thatch was kept free of bugs by the peat smoke, but in rainy weather it tended to drip sooty water onto the house's inhabitants. Until recently, few houses had windows, though again the better-off had them put in, as far back as the Norse period.

It is unrealistic to romanticise the quality of life in Orcadian longhouses – equally it is important not to think of that life as primitive and brutish. The longhouse was a very sound structure which made ingenious use of the available raw materials, and its design gave complete protection from Orkney's penetrating winds and bleak winter weather. It was a snug

Flagstone cupboards, an ale-hurry or shelf and a goose nest at floor level in an old Orkney longhouse

home, roomier and most certainly warmer than many of the rather flimsy 'executive-type' homes thrown up in recent times by speculative builders in the south. Many longhouses have been modernised in the present century by re-plastering and papering the walls, by inserting windows and replacing the central hearth with a stove. Flagstone fitted furniture was sometimes disguised with paint and cupboard-linings.

TRADITIONAL DIET

What did people eat and drink in the old Orkney farmhouses? The traditional Orkney foods would seem monotonous to us, but they were nutritious, and there was some variation through the year according to the raw materials available. Potatoes and various forms of porridge or thick grain

soup were the mainstays. Potatoes were prepared in a variety of ways; porridge and soups were made from bere or oatmeal. Bere meal was also made into bread and bannocks, though the latter were extremely hard because there was no baking powder nor any of the other modern ingredients which are added to today's 'traditional' bannocks. This starchy basic diet was supplemented in season with cabbage, turnips, kale and other vegetables, helped down with a little fresh milk, butter and cheese from the household cow. Eggs were fairly plentiful; there were always hens running around an Orkney farmhouse. However, butcher's meat was a rarity because of the storage problem: it was eaten on Sundays by the better-off, but only on special occasions by the majority, and comprised salt pork, smoked

A restored longhouse living room at Corrigall Farm Museum

goose, and beef in autumn when cattle had to be slaughtered because of the shortage of winter feed. Smoked mutton, sausage and haggis were produced from the native long-tailed sheep.

Fish was sometimes available, but not everyone could afford it. Especially valuable was the sardine-like sillock, which came in shoals to Orkney from time to time and which yielded fresh and dried fish and a nutritious oil. On some of the outer islands, local men risked life and limb to gather seabirds' eggs and to net the birds themselves on the Faroese principle. For seasoning, salt and pepper were available, but there was almost no sugar. As to drink, every house stood near a spring, while bere was used to brew ale. An unpublicised amount of whisky distilling was also practised.

FARMING METHODS UNREFORMED

AS TO THE TRADITIONAL farming methods which went with the old houses, almost no visible signs remain in Orkney's very twentieth-century countryside. Fortunately we have some detailed accounts of the old ways of farming, while collections of traditional farm implements are preserved at Tankerness House and the two farm museums.

Farming methods were primitive in Orkney right up until the eighteenth and nineteenth centuries, when a few reforming estate owners introduced new crops such as wild white clover, improved breeds of livestock and new methods. It is no exaggeration to say that farming practices which would have been familiar to the Vikings were to be observed in parts of Orkney as late as the mid-nineteenth century, to the astonishment of visitors. Before these improvements, land was undrained and full of weeds. Ploughing was done with a single-stilt plough, a particularly ineffectual instrument. Its use is vividly described by Daniel Gorrie:

Dounby click-mill, an example of a small water-mill for grinding grain. Orkney traditionally exported grain to the Highlands, produced from mills such as this

'The old Orkney plough was single-stilted and wanted a mould-board. It was drawn by three and sometimes four ponies or oxen, which were yoked abreast and had their heads fastened to a beam of wood. The driver, grasping this piece of wood with one hand and his whip with the other, walked backwards in front of the animals; and the ploughman, following up in the rear, leant his weight against one side of the instrument, occasionally using a pattle-tree to clear away clods, or hasten the pace of his refractory team. All this expenditure of energy was quite superfluous, as the plough only scratched the surface of the fields, and the trampling of so many feet and hooves poached the soil when soft, and hardened it when dry . . . '

The plough was followed by a harrow with wooden teeth, which 'served only to comb the ground that had previously been scratched'.

It was well-nigh impossible to improve cultivation methods because of the way the land was divided. All plough land was split up into narrow strips called rigs, and these rigs were allocated to tenant farmers in a complicated way, the purpose of which was to share out all the different qualities of land equally. Since most of the land was equally bad, in practice the system served only to delay improvement. In each township, the senior

The Corrigall Farm Museum site before restoration: longhouse with parallel byre and barn, medieval water-mill and remains of an Iron Age broch

family received the most northerly and westerly rig, the next-senior family the next rig, and so on until a first allocation had been made to all families; then the process was repeated until all the land had been taken up. Each 'farm' therefore consisted of a series of narrow strips separated by other tenants' strips. Until this so-called run-rig land had been consolidated into fields, improvements in cultivation methods were impossible.

Livestock management was also haphazard: cattle and sheep roamed the unfenced common lands in summer, and no attempt was made to control breeding or to improve stock in other ways. In winter the animals were brought off the hill and inside the head-dyke which surrounded the cultivated land; this resulted in a lot of trampling and poaching which further reduced soil quality.

This was the situation up to the very beginning of modern times; but already there were a few estate owners in Orkney who knew what to do to make things better. The appearance of Orkney's countryside today is mainly the result of what they did.

6 MODERN TIMES

TWO THINGS HAD TO BE DONE before Orkney farming could be modernised; first, the run-rig system had to be swept away; and second, the people who actually worked the land had to be given the incentive to improve their properties and do more than the absolute minimum of work. Rather like the collective farm operatives in the former Soviet Union, Orkney tenants had no rights and therefore no sense of responsibility or desire to do things better.

A first attempt at enclosing the run-rig was made in 1760 when the so-called first planking of the land took place. This achieved very little because of lack of capital and interference by those with vested interests, and the mosaic of small plots which resulted was no more workable than the run-rig. The second and successful planking began in the 1830s and took thirty years to complete, and it transformed the Orkney countryside into the regular pattern of fields we see today. This radical redistribution of the land was

Binscarth, a fine example of a mid-nineteenth century reforming estate. The final 'planking' of Orkney's farmland into workable units began here

Boardhouse estate mill in Birsay, Orkney's last mill to survive in full working order

pushed through by enlightened estate owners who at long last had a market for their produce in the emerging industrial towns of the south; they could also now reach these markets by virtue of the first regular steamer services, which began in the 1830s. The first estate to be planked at this time was Binscarth, between Finstown and Maes Howe.

As the nineteenth century advanced, the Orkney estates built up a substantial export trade in beef cattle, sheep and eggs. The cattle were mainly Shorthorns and polled Angus, which produced high quality meat; by the 1860s, more than 10,000 beasts were being shipped out each year to the Aberdeen marts. Also, Merino and Southdown sheep were introduced and crossed with the hardy island breed to produce enormously more productive animals; as a result sheep numbers fell dramatically, though the output of meat and wool climbed steadily.

The rise in the egg business was truly spectacular. Hens had always been kept on Orkney farms, but now they became the basis of a whole new export industry – by 1900 Orkney was shipping out more than a million dozen eggs annually. According to custom, looking after the chickens had always been the responsibility of farmers' wives and now they kept the profits from the egg business; many household improvements were paid for out of the egg earnings. Feedstuffs had to be imported, but they were cheap at a time of low farm prices.

Orkney households had always ground bere for private use. Then in the eighteenth and even more in the nineteenth centuries, progressive estate owners built up an export business in bere and barley to the Highlands, an area which suffered persistent grain shortages. Many new mills were built at this time and their remains still dot the Orkney countryside. Only one such mill remains in full working order, Boardhouse in Birsay, as has already been noted. Tormiston Mill, opposite Maes Howe, closed in 1961 and has since been converted into an attractive restaurant and craft centre; it makes a good base from which to explore West Mainland.

A unique example of a much smaller type of mill is to be seen in Dounby: worked by a horizontal water-wheel set over a stream, this so-called click-mill is reminiscent of small watermills of medieval design which could be seen working in western Norway until the 1960s.

SECURITY OF TENURE

RIGHTS FOR TENANTS came after 1886, through the work of the Crofting Commission, chaired by Lord Napier. This commission transformed the situation of tenants throughout northern Scotland, and the legislation which resulted created a new legal entity, the crofter. Crofters were estate tenants who were granted what amounted to an absolute right to retain their land and to pass it to their descendants. Strict regulations governed the maximum size of their holdings and the uses to which land might be put; rents were fixed, but very much to the tenants' advantage. At last tenants had both security and an incentive to improve their properties.

For the estate owners, on the other hand, commercial survival hence-forth depended upon there being profitable markets for their products, and so there were, until the great agricultural depression which followed World War I – then it transpired that the Crofting Commission had driven a very big nail indeed into the coffin of the Orkney estate system.

FROM TENANT TO OWNER-FARMER

TWO WORLD WARS ensured that Orkney farms made money; moreover from 1914 to 1919, Scapa Flow was the principal Royal Navy base in the north, and the great fleet and its supporting personnel had to be fed. Orkney crofters did the job, and because of the low fixed rents, pocketed most of the profits. So when the great farming depression began and many estate owners found that their properties were valueless, tenants had enough money to buy their holdings, usually at a price equivalent to twenty-three years' annual rent. Most tenants had to raise loans for part of this sum, and then spent the next quarter century paying them back; however, they were able to do this because they were in effect almost self-sufficient in basic foodstuffs and could buy imported feeds at very low prices. This was a time of very hard graft for Orkney's country people.

Then in 1939 another huge market presented itself: at the start of World War II the fleet returned to Scapa and because of the threat of invasion, a garrison was built up which at times numbered over 60,000 men and women. Feeding this multitude, even at low wartime prices, was very profitable indeed and most mortgages on farms were paid off at this time. By 1945 or soon after, Orkney's farmers were established as independent smallholders, ready to take advantage of the market opportunities of the post-war years. Thus Orkney became the land of owner-farmers we see today.

FIFTY YEARS ON

Orkney's 'planked' landscape, very fertile after draining and devoted to grass, beef and dairy cattle and in the foreground, seed potatoes

THE POST WAR YEARS have generally been good for Orkney. The islands' beef cattle producers have built up the amount and quality of their production, supported by favourable subsidies. Oil was discovered under the North sea and Flotta was selected as a principal terminal site for bringing it ashore. The tourist industry has grown steadily and learned how to market the riches of the islands' archaeology and natural history to discerning visitors. Fortunately there will never be a mass market for burial cairns and birds!

Dairy herds were built up during World War II, and they have been maintained to service the requirements of cheese-making and the output of other milk-based products; there is of course no possibility of shipping milk regularly across the Pentland Firth. On the other hand egg production, which was so very profitable in its time, succumbed to the competition of battery producers in the south who were nearer to markets and able to bargain for huge discounts on their bulk feedstuffs.

ORKNEY AND THE BEEF MOUNTAIN

TRADITIONALLY ORKNEY has concentrated its energies upon the least profitable end of the beef business, the production of live animals for export 'on the hoof'; only in the 1970s was an abattoir built at Kirkwall to produce finished meat for export. This coincided with the long-promised introduction of a ro-ro ferry on the Stromness–Scrabster route, allowing container lorries to drive to and from the British mainland, though at a cost.

Unfortunately these developments were accompanied by four major problems for beef producers: the continual rise in meat prices; changing eating habits, with a new emphasis upon vegetarianism; the accumulation

Backaskaill, an example of a large nineteenth century reforming estate in the north isle of Sanday

of a huge beef surplus in the then-European Community, known as the beef mountain; and worries about so-called 'mad cow' disease. All four of these difficulties continue, especially that of surplus production in Europe caused by subsidies which are less and less justifiable year by year. By the late 1990s, the European Union's tax-payers were spending £1.08 billion each year in buying beef from farmers and holding it in cold-store; beef subsidies were by then the largest of all EU agricultural subsidies. Needless to say, this situation will not be allowed to continue, and ways will be found of reducing the surplus and cutting production. However, it remains to be seen how the inevitable cuts in subsidy will affect Orkney's farmers.

Other aspects of Orkney's economy suffer from competition from major producers which are sometimes subsidised – salmon fisheries are a case in point. Orcadians have invested heavily in salmon farming in recent years, only to find their position undermined by the alleged dumping of cheaper Norwegian salmon on the European market. Recently frozen salmon from Chile has begun to pose a further threat to Scottish salmon farmers.

OIL AND ORKNEY

OIL REVENUES have been a tremendous help to Orkney. They have been skilfully managed by the Orkney Islands Council and used to hold down rates and other charges, thus counteracting the continual rise in transport costs to the south. Internal ferries between islands have been subsidised; education, healthcare and other aspects of the islands' infrastructure have also benefited, and there has been some money for the arts and tourism.

As with beef, however, the future of oil in Orkney is uncertain. Occidental Oil sold its Flotta terminal to the nationalised French company, Elf-Aquitaine in 1991. In 1994 this company was sold off to private investors, mainly large financial institutions in Europe. Elf operates in a world of persistent oil surpluses and falling revenues and in the 1990s it began to make great efforts to drive down its production costs by reducing its labour force. Job losses began at Flotta exactly twenty years after the terminal was begun.

The future of Flotta depends upon where new sources of oil and gas are developed. There are still large reserves under the North Sea, and also out on the continental shelf west of Orkney and Shetland, where the seas are deeper. The question is, will these reserves be exploited or will investment move to cheaper sources, in for example the Russian Sub-Arctic, the Black Sea, the Mediterranean and the Middle East? Flotta's future will depend upon decisions made far away from Orkney at the global scale.

Amidst all the uncertainties, Orkney has one great advantage, that of political stability; some of the cheaper alternative sites certainly do not have this. Furthermore Orkney is securely within the European Union. For these reasons, it seems likely that Flotta terminal will still be operating fifty years from now.

7 STROMNESS AND THE NORTHERN SEA ROUTES

STROMNESS STANDS on the arm of the sea called Hamla Voe, sometimes spelled Hamnavoe, in West Mainland. This haven has been used since the beginning of history by ships seeking shelter from Atlantic storms, and more recently as a way-station for northern voyages, to Scandinavia, the Baltic and the Americas. As it appears today the town is little more than two centuries old, but commercial activity developed along the Hamla Voe shore much earlier. Stromness is famous in Scottish history as the rising small town whose merchants successfully challenged the commercial monopoly of the royal burghs in the mid-eighteenth century. It is also one of the most picturesque small towns in Scotland.

Stromness roofscape: a single winding street along the shore of Hamla Voe, the Hoy hills beyond

Logically a visit to Stromness begins at Login's Well, situated towards the south end of the town's single main street. Water from this well has been used from time immemorial to supply visiting ships; ample sources of good drinking water have always been hard to find. The value of the well and the great advantages of Hamla Voe as a safe haven were recognised by the Hudson's Bay Company in 1670. From then until 1891 the company's ships came here every year to take on supplies and fresh water ready for their voyage to Arctic Canada. Even after their Stromness base was closed, the company continued to order stores here until 1914.

Login's Well, valued source of drinking water for ships taking the hazardous northabout route around Britain

Because of the Hudson Bay connection, many hundreds of Orcadians had the chance to work in Canada; between sixty and one hundred were usually employed there at any one time. Most served as labourers, but no less than ten became governors or chief factors of the company; another eighteen achieved the rank of district master or chief trader. By 1750 the Hudson's Bay agent in Stromness was paying out about £3,000 in wages annually; most of the recruits came from the Stromness area and consequently farms were often neglected. Today the Hudson's Bay Company still recruits staff from time to time through advertisements in *The Orcadian* newspaper.

Under the terms of its royal charter, the Hudson's Bay Company was required to explore and map its arctic territories. One of its most distinguished navigators and explorers was Dr John Rae, whose monument has been noted in St Magnus' Cathedral. John Rae made five voyages to the Arctic between 1846 and 1854, adding more than one thousand miles (1,600km) of new coastline to the charts. He also ascertained the probable fate of Sir John Franklin's expedition, which vanished in 1847 during an attempt to sail through the North-West Passage. Franklin had watered his ships, *Erebus* and *Terror* from Login's Well in the spring of 1845. The 1993 Cambridge Arctic Expedition located what appeared to be the wreck of one of Franklin's boats. Eventually the full story of Franklin's great voyage may be known.

From about 1760 until the 1830s, Hamla Voe and its fresh water were regularly used by the Davis Strait whalers. These vessels set out in March to hunt the Greenland whales which were then abundant, and both whales and their pursuers followed the retreating ice northwards. As stocks declined, the whalers had to penetrate further and further into more and more perilous waters. Eventually over-fishing reduced the stocks dramatically and the Greenland whaling industry collapsed.

A busy scene in Stromness harbour

Right: Stromness: morning calm. The house on the left was originally built for army officers stationed here during the Napoleonic wars

These events marked the beginnings of Stromness; but it was the Napoleonic Wars which put the town firmly on the map. During these protracted wars, the English Channel was often hazardous for commercial shipping; and so vessels bound for ports in North Germany, the Baltic, Russia and Scandinavia took to using the northabout route around Britain. This route has always been used when the more comfortable southerly sea passages were made dangerous by pirates and privateers, as they were in Jacobite times. The northabout route took ships west of St Kilda and north of the Butt of Lewis, then east through the Pentland Firth or Sumburgh Roost, sometimes north of Shetland itself. Though stormy and bereft of lighthouses, this route was relatively safe because it kept to open water. However, a secure way-station was needed along it and Stromness was ideal for the purpose; as more and more ships called, the town grew quickly and a garrison was soon added to protect it from sea raiders. The house built for the garrison's officers still stands near the battery towards the town's south end, while the walls on Brinkie's Brae, the hill behind the town, were mostly built by the soldiers to keep them busy.

Stromness is a Napoleonic boom-town and it still looks like one, though its houses are no doubt better maintained and more attractively painted than they were then.

Part of the mile-long street

Right: Stromness: ship at the end of the pier. The mv Fingal *services lighthouses and buoys around the Scottish coast from its Stromness base*

THE QUOYS

THE TOWN has one principal winding, stone-flagged street, more or less parallel with the shore. The older properties were built end-on to the street; those on the shoreward side run down to small private piers. The first house on each of these long and narrow properties would be built on the shore, then outbuildings and newer houses would be built behind them. A vacant piece of land would be left between the back of the first house and its outbuildings and the front of the next; and these vacant plots were eventually joined up to make the present irregular street. The long narrow properties ending at the shore were called quoys. Narrow alleys run between some of them, giving picturesque views of the town from the shore. On the inland side of the street, steep passages such as the Khyber Pass lead to the upper town and the hill.

Few of the old houses have any special architectural distinction, but they do have a unity of style and scale which is very pleasing. Some are dated; most are from the Napoleonic boom years, though there is some limited Victorian and Edwardian development near the pier, such as the imposing Stromness Hotel built in 1901. Outside this closely-knit core there are many newer properties. The population is now just above 3,000, an increase of a third since World War II.

Stromness boasts a very fine Arts Centre at the pierhead, also a museum with a fine collection of items relating to the town's history; and a good library, with much local material. Stromness Academy is now located in new premises outside the old town and is Orkney's second secondary school, with a fine tradition of educating young Orcadians. The town is also home to one of Britain's most distinguished poets and writers, George Mackay Brown. Mr Brown's books and poems are based upon a profound knowledge of Orcadian life and they should certainly be read by anyone who wishes to understand Orkney and its people. Those who feel unable to tackle the *Orkneyinga Saga* itself will find his novel *Vinland* (1992) an evocative introduction to those stirring times.

Stromness has a good golf-course, with a striking backdrop of the Hoy hills across Hoy Sound. At the pierhead, boats may be hired for a crossing to Hoy, Orkney's best island for hill walking.

8 SCAPA FLOW

The land-locked waters of Scapa Flow
are central to this map of Orkney,
produced for the New Statistical
Account of 1842

S CAPA FLOW is one of Britain's most historic expanses of water. It
was a naval base in both world wars and might be thought of as the
Pearl Harbour of the north. The south isles which enclose it to the
east offer fine views across the Flow and have several interesting
places to visit.

NAVIES IN THE NORTH

SHIPS HAVE USED the sheltered waters of Scapa Flow since prehistory, but
the Flow became nationally important this century when Kaiser Wilhelm's
Germany engaged in a race with Britain for naval supremacy. The British
Admiralty knew, that in the event of war, it must be able to stop the Kaiser's
warships slipping out into the Atlantic to cut off Britain's seaborne supplies.
It therefore looked for a fleet base in the north and found Scapa ideal for the
purpose, largely because it offers good anchoring conditions and is big
enough to shelter an entire navy at once. So a major base was established,
which remained in use until 1956. Today, occasional NATO exercises are
held in the Flow.

There is little by way of relics or remains from World War I since many
of the supporting installations were seaborne because of the lack of facilities
on shore. At Lyness, however, major installations were built, some of them
below ground; and the remains of this base have lately been developed into
a museum which tells the story of Scapa in the two world wars.

The fleet sailed in May 1916 from Scapa to fight the battle of Jutland,
which the survivors of both sides believed they had won. This was the last
time two fleets engaged in a set-piece battle in the style of Nelson's day, and
the consequences were catastrophic for both. Modern guns did untold
damage to life and limb, and amply demonstrated the out-moded nature of
this kind of warfare. Although Jutland was nobody's victory, the Kaiser's
fleet never ventured to sea again, and for the remainder of the war, naval
actions mostly involved submarines and submarine hunters.

Most of the British sailors posted to Scapa Flow found life boring
almost beyond endurance; though just occasionally something notable did
happen. One such incident came in June 1916 when Lord Kitchener, the
commander-in-chief and a national hero and father-figure, arrived in
Scapa on his way to St Petersburg; his mission was to encourage the Czar and

his generals to stay in the war. After dining on board the Admiral's flagship, Kitchener and his staff transferred to the cruiser HMS *Hampshire*. The ship put to sea through Hoy Sound, to be sunk almost immediately, probably by mines, perhaps by a U-boat, possibly by some other means. Whatever the cause, the *Hampshire* sank with remarkable speed, and the few who survived found their way ashore in Birsay and were told to say nothing about what had happened. Perhaps it was feared that news of Kitchener's death would cause panic. In fact history suggests that his loss was a blessing in disguise so far as the conduct of the war was concerned. After the war, a large and undistinguished monument was raised to Kitchener's memory on the Birsay cliffs.

At the armistice, seventy-four ships of the Kaiser's navy were ordered into Scapa Flow to surrender. They arrived, a fine sight, in November 1918. For the next six months the ships lay at anchor, manned by skeleton crews who were fed inadequately direct from Germany and who became steadily more mutinous; roller-skating round the decks of the larger ships became a favourite pastime. Then in June 1919 the peace terms were at last announced and were staggeringly severe. It is thought that the German commanding officer at Scapa saw the terms in *The Times* and forthwith decided to scuttle the whole fleet as a final act of defiance. This was done, watched as it happened by a school party out from Stromness to view the ships: it must have been the most exciting school outing of all time!

Silent waters. Scapa Flow from the Hoy hills, powdered with late-winter snow. Ferries, tankers and the occasional pleasure craft now ply these waters where whole navies once lay at anchor

An incident with a much more pleasant outcome had occurred a month earlier when Harry Hawker and Mackenzie Grieve made their epic attempt to fly the Atlantic non-stop. Their single-engined Sopwith monoplane was forced down by torrential rain, fortunately close to a Danish ship – though as luck would have it, this particular ship had no radio, an eventuality which by then was unusual. As it was 1,000km (600 miles) out from Scotland, news of the rescue was long delayed – a memorial service was even planned for the two aviators in Westminster Abbey, though Hawker's wife steadfastly refused to believe he was lost. Then the Danish ship arrived off the Butt of Lewis and semaphored to the lighthouse that she had picked up two aviators in mid-Atlantic. Laboriously the message was spelled out, to be interrupted by the question, Is it Hawker? Slowly came the answer, Yes. News of the rescue was telegraphed to London, where it is said that the editor of *The Times* sent for a reporter and told him to take a taxi to the Butt of Lewis to get the full story. More practically, Admiral Beattie, commanding the fleet in Scapa Flow, sent a destroyer to bring the two airmen to Orkney. After being fêted on board his flagship, they were sent off to London by train; and at every station, so it is said, they were given a triumphal reception. A month later, Alcock and Brown became the first men to fly the Atlantic non-stop in a heavier-than-air machine. This was an exciting time for aviation 'firsts'.

The St George of Camp 60, the Italian prisoner-of-war camp, made out of coiled barbed wire and cement in the 1940s

SIXTY THOUSAND VISITORS IN ORKNEY: WORLD WAR II

WAR RE-STARTED IN 1939 with two dramatic reminders of Scapa Flow's new vulnerability in the current age of airpower and much-improved submarines. First came an air raid in the course of which the first British civilian was killed near the bridge of Waithe near Stromness; a redundant World War I battleship, HMS *Iron Duke*, was also sunk. Then on 14 October the battleship HMS *Royal Oak* was torpedoed as she lay at anchor under the cliffs of Gaitnip; a Nazi submarine had managed to slip through the incomplete defences of the Flow and out again without being detected. About eight hundred men perished that night. Their remains lie under the waters of the Flow, and together with their ship are protected by a great steel net; the site is designated a war grave and divers are asked to respect its privacy. A buoy marks the spot.

Following these attacks, the Royal Navy used Scapa with caution. The new emphasis was upon forestalling a possible invasion of the North Isles, and so a huge garrison was built up in Orkney which at its peak numbered more than 60,000 men and women, army, Air Force and navy. The garrison was housed in camps, most of which have been cleared away; but part of one remains, the Ness Battery Camp near Stromness, which can be used by school and student groups. Around the dining hall are murals painted by a Mr Wood in the course of dark Orkney winters, country scenes from the

Second Churchill Barrier, one of four built during World War II to protect the Flow from U-boats and improve communications to the South Isles of Burray and South Ronaldsay

Italian prisoners-of-war from the Dolomites built this chapel out of two Nissen huts during their stay in Orkney

south with thatched cottages, trees and flowers – they are not great art, but are deeply evocative of those grim years in Britain's history when so many people from the south came unwillingly to Orkney. In happier times, some of these returned, having learned to enjoy these northern islands where they had been compulsory visitors.

THE ITALIAN CHAPEL
AND THE CHURCHILL BARRIERS

IMMEDIATELY SOUTH OF GAITNIP where the *Royal Oak* went down are the Churchill Barriers or causeways, linking Orkney Mainland with the South Isles of Burray and South Ronaldsay, by way of two small islets. On one of these, Lamb's Holm, stands the Italian Chapel, one of Orkney's famous tourist sites. It was built by Italian prisoners-of-war who were brought here from the Western Desert after General Wavell's defeat of Il

Duce's Army in 1940. They were housed in Camp 60, and were employed from time to time in helping to build the Churchill Barriers, the main function of which was to cut out the tiresome ferry journey between Mainland and the South Isles. In fact they have probably saved these isles from post-war depopulation.

A group of talented Italians decided to build a chapel, using two standard Nissen huts as a base. They used waste materials taken from redundant vehicles and obsolete military equipment, and produced a work of true ingenuity and imagination. Domenico Chiocchetti, who came from Moena, painted the interior in a striking *tromp l'oeil* style; after the war he was invited back to Orkney to touch up his handiwork. The chapel is used for Roman Catholic services and is very well worth a visit. Those who come to Orkney by the John O'Groats ferry pass on it their way to Kirkwall.

OIL IN SCAPA FLOW

THE SMALL ISLAND OF FLOTTA in Scapa Flow is a major base for the North Sea oil industry. In the early days after the discovery of oil beneath the North Sea, there was a period of great confusion; it seemed possible that individual land owners in Orkney might be picked off by competing oil interests from outside, to the detriment of the community as a whole. Advised by their distinguished Member of Parliament, Jo Grimond, later Lord Grimond, the Orkney Islands Council succeeded in establishing the principle that they alone would negotiate with outside companies about oil-related matters. In 1974 they granted planning permission to one major company, Occidental, to establish a pipeline terminal and processing installation on the island of Flotta, where depopulation had reached such an advanced stage that total collapse of the community was imminent. The terminal has since passed into the ownership of Elf-Aquitaine.

The Flotta terminal receives crude oil from several fields to the east, a pipeline bringing their combined outputs across South Ronaldsay and so to Flotta. On arrival it is very cold and has first to be warmed to a working temperature before processing can begin; methane, which is included with the oil, is used for the purpose. The oil and gases such as methane, ethane and propane (Calor gas) are separated, then stored for onward shipment by tanker; huge tankers are thus a familiar sight in the southern part of the Flow – in a typical week, six or seven will leave Flotta for ports in Germany, Scandinavia, the Netherlands, Spain, Portugal and occasionally Britain. Many tankers fly flags of convenience; the red ensign is rarely seen these days in the Flow.

WHALES IN THE FLOW

The first Orkney Book, *edited by John Gunn in 1909 and published by Thomas Nelson, included a chapter about whale-hunting written by Daniel Gorrie some sixty years earlier. The trapping and beaching of whales in bays used to be a well-established practice in the Faroe Islands and to a lesser extent in Shetland and Orkney.*

Today, whales which become trapped in shallow water among islands are more likely to be shepherded out to sea by a fleet of small boats. This happened in March 1993 when six sperm whales became trapped in Scapa Flow, unable to find their way out.

On 25 March, an armada, which included the harbour tugs, the pilot boat, boats belonging to Elf Oil and Orkney Seal Rescue, fishing boats, private craft and inflatables from the Sea Mammal Research Unit, supported by a spotter 'plane, assembled near Flotta. The whales were successfully urged through the narrows off Hoxa and were last seen swimming into the open ocean, none the worse for a month's confinement in the Flow

9 ORKNEY'S NATURAL HISTORY

A NYTHING APPROACHING a full account of Orkney's rich and varied natural history would take up several books; indeed it already has. All that can be done here is to indicate the best sources of detailed information, to outline the main characteristics of the islands' fauna and flora, and to suggest a few locations which are well worth visiting.

Further information about every aspect of Orkney's natural history is abundant. For more than a century Orkney has been producing experts in many fields, and these experts have written books and papers about almost every aspect of the islands' wildlife. Some of the most important titles are listed in the bibliography at the end of this book and they may be consulted at Orkney's public libraries.

The Orkney Field Club (OFC) is another important point of contact for interested visitors. It is a body of private enthusiasts, and since its foundation in 1959 has built up a formidable body of expertise about Orkney's natural history. It publishes an ever-growing list of newsletters, survey reports and biological records and since 1994 has produced a regular journal. Month-by-month bird sightings are included in its publications and it is busy establishing a computerised database of all wildlife information. Membership of the OFC is open to people from outside Orkney and visitors are always welcome at its meetings; note that enquiries addressed to the club should always be accompanied by a stamped and addressed envelope. The Royal Society for the Protection of Birds (RSPB) has representatives in Orkney; while the British Butterfly Conservation Society (BBCS) includes Orkney in its Highland Region. The Orkney Tourist Board publishes leaflets which describe aspects of the islands' wildlife, also guide leaflets to the various islands which include wildlife information.

The tiny Primula Scotica, *confined to Orkney, Sutherland and Caithness, is to be found in several clifftop locations. It flowers in June*

MARGINAL ENVIRONMENTS, MIGRANTS AND MUTATIONS

Marsh-marigolds grow in damp sites in many parts of Orkney

A primrose bank, sure sign that spring has come after a long, wet winter

CHIEF AMONG THE INFLUENCES which have shaped Orkney's wildlife populations are the distance north; access to the ocean and nearness to migration tracks; strong winds which sometimes blow birds and insects to Orkney from far afield; and the development of sub-species in isolation. This latter development is characteristic of all islands in which species have been isolated in small numbers over long periods of time.

Hoy is Orkney's greatest treasure-house of plants. The only native trees in Orkney live here, sheltered from salt-laden winds and grazing animals in the narrow clefts, called glens, which descend from the slopes of Ward Hill, the Cuilags and the island's other northern hills. Species include rowan, hazel, birch, aspen and sallow. Corries such as the Nowt Bield contain rare alpines. Here too are sudden reminders of the rise in sea-level which cut off Orkney from Scotland at the end of the Ice Age. There is no bog myrtle *(Myrica gale)* in Hoy, though it is common in Sutherland. Strangely, the plant does live in Eday. The explanation for this curious distribution may be that the plant only just managed to reach Orkney before the rising sea-level turned the land into islands; and that the more extreme climatic conditions on the Hoy hills compared with the more sheltered Eday, wiped out the small toe-hold colonies which had been established at the edge of their range. Moorland fires could

The Painted Lady butterfly, a powerful migrant, is a summer visitor to Orkney

The Small Copper butterfly is a rare visitor to Hoy from its northern colony in Caithness

Right: wood at Westness, Rousay. Small woods such as this give shelter from the persistent winds to a wide variety of flora and fauna

also have played a part in the extinction; the Hoy hills are susceptible to widespread fires in dry weather.

Sand-dunes at the Bay of Skaill, on the island of Sanday and elsewhere have rich assemblages of plants; the blue-flowered oyster plant is a fine rarity. Angelica, which looks something like hogweed but flowers later in the year, is thought to have been introduced by the Norse settlers and may be found here and there, in Deerness for example. Given shelter from the all-pervasive winds, a great variety of plants will grow in Orkney; there are some fine gardens, private and public, which show what can be done.

Orkney's most notable insect is the midge, which can be a sore trial on the hills when the weather is still, warm and damp. The hills of North Hoy are a stronghold for this penetrating creature and visitors should never venture there in summer without a supply of midge repellent – even the hill summits have midges.

Butterflies and moths *(lepidoptera)* are surprisingly well represented, considering the high latitude and exposure. They have been the subject of intensive study in recent years and unusual species are continually being observed, mainly immigrants from the south. For instance 1992 was the year of the convolvulus hawk moth *(Sphinx convolvuli)*, of which there were a remarkable number of sightings; in that summer too, the clouded yellow *(Colias croceus)* butterfly reached Orkney in considerable numbers. Powerful migrants such as the red admiral *(Vanessa atalanta)* and painted lady *(Cynthia cardui)* come into Orkney regularly but cannot establish themselves. Species which are very common

further south, such as the small white *(Pieris rapae)*, are almost unknown in Orkney. The small copper *(Lycaena phlaeas)*, of which a colony exists in Caithness, is occasionally blown across to Hoy but does not seem able to survive an Orkney winter.

ORKNEY'S BIRDS

BIRDS ARE THE MOST publicised glory of Orkney's wildlife and undoubted tourist attractions. The whole Atlantic coast of Hoy is lined with bird-cliffs where visitors may see a profusion of gulls, guillemots, terns, kittiwakes, oyster-catchers, cormorants, shags and skuas (called *bonxies* in Orkney). The whole area of hill inland from the Old Man of Hoy is in the care of the RSPB, and there is an RSPB resident officer in Hoy.

Other fine seabird localities are to be found along the Atlantic coast of Mainland and in the North Isles. The Noup Head cliffs on Westray are second only to St Kilda for the numbers of seabirds which breed there; the area has been designated a Site of Special Scientific Interest (SSSI) and is of international scientific importance. Other breeding cliffs are to be found on Papa Westray, the Calf of Eday, the south coasts of Stronsay and the east coasts of Shapinsay. It is interesting to note that Papa Westray was the last home of the great auk, a splendid bird which was shot to extinction in 1913; the last specimen is in the South Kensington Natural History Museum.

Migrant species may be seen, especially on Sanday, North Ronaldsay and Eday, from March to June at the start of the year, and from August to November at the year's end.

Orkney has many splendid bird cliffs, like this one near Noup Head in Westray

Left: bird cliff on the Brough of Birsay. Almost every known species of sea bird visits Orkney's sandstone cliffs in the course of a year

ORKNEY'S ANIMALS

THE MOST UNUSUAL of Orkney's small animals is the Orkney vole (*Microtus orcadensis*). This is a unique sub-species of the European vole (*Microtus arvalis*) found in the British Isles only in Orkney and in Guernsey. Its extraordinary distribution probably indicates that the tiny animal reached Orkney in the wake of the retreating ice, that its colonies were then cut off, and that they continued to evolve and mutate in isolation so that the distinctive characteristics of a few individuals were emphasised.

Unique sub-species are to be found in many island groups throughout the world. One is reminded of the puzzling presence of what looks like the Indian form of the red admiral butterfly (*Vanessa indica vulcania*) in the Canary Islands and its absence from nearby Africa. Possibly this, too, is a mutation in an isolated island environment.

Colourful lichens grow in Orkney's porous sandstones

Other animals of interest include the alpine or blue hare, reintroduced into Hoy in the eighteenth century after a long absence; it flourishes on the north Hoy moors. It changes its coat to white in winter whether there is snow on the ground or not, and is often highly conspicuous, a white fleck against a background of dark-brown heather and grass. The common hare was also an introduced animal, but was wiped out by hunting.

Long-tailed fieldmice were probably brought in by Norse immigrants with their food and bedding. How is it possible to know this? The answer lies in slight peculiarities in their bone structure, which show them to be more closely related to Norwegian than to Scottish mice. Research by Professor R. J. Berry and others has demonstrated these Viking links in Shetland, St Kildan and Hebridean long-tailed mice, and there is a high probability that they also exist in Orkney's mouse population. Another introduction is the hedgehog, brought to Orkney by a minister's sons in the 1870s and topped up with further introductions during World War II.

As to native Orkney animals – that is, those which managed to reach Orkney before the rising sea-level cut them off – the most important survivors are otters, toads, the house mouse, pygmy shrews and rabbits. Other species have not survived; these include the red deer, reindeer, wolf, badger, fox and wild boar. Some species never reached Orkney: there are no frogs, newts or adders in the islands.

Left: Birsay rock-pool. Seas around Orkney are relatively warm and there is rich marine life in localities sheltered from wave attack

10 AN INNER NORTHERN CIRCUIT

ROUSAY, EGILSAY, WYRE AND SHAPINSAY are the most easily visited of the North Isles, and are accessible by day excursions from Mainland. The ferry for the first three islands leaves from Tingwall pier, that for Shapinsay from Kirkwall harbour. Private boat trips can also be arranged by consulting the Orkney Tourist Board.

ROUSAY

ROUSAY is an almost circular island, farmed around the edges and with a moorland centre. It has a quite astonishing array of ancient monuments, all of them on the slopes facing Mainland.

Working west from Trumland pier, the usual landing place, the first Neolithic cairn stands in a commanding position above the road: this is Taversoe Tuick, in its way as remarkable as Maes Howe. Fortunately the existence of this cairn was unsuspected until 1898, in which year the then-proprietor of Trumland estate decided to have a lookout seat erected at this point. The upper chamber of the cairn was then revealed but no further digging was done. When scientific excavation was carried out in 1937 for the Ministry of Public Buildings and Works, the cairn was revealed as a two-decker structure, having a subterranean lower chamber and a stone-built upper chamber. There was no connection between the two, though both were enclosed within a circular wall. The lower chamber only contained a few interments and some fragments of Onston-type pottery, suggesting its use from a very early date. The two-decker arrangement probably denotes that burials continued here over a very long period.

Further west again is Blackhammer cairn, a well-preserved Neolithic burial chamber of the stalled type. Higher up the hill is Yarso cairn, again of the stalled type, which on excavation yielded the remains of twenty-one people, also the bones of red deer and many pottery fragments. Dates calculated by Colin Renfrew and others for the use of this cairn suggest that it was open for burials from around 3300 to 2100BC. Once again, the extreme difficulty of giving precise dates for Neolithic monuments has to be emphasised. Readers who have a particular interest in these investigations are invited to consult the research reports for more detailed analyses of the findings.

Left: Midhowe stalled cairn in Rousay is one of Orkney's most remarkable pre-historic monuments. Human bones were interred in the stone compartments on either side of a central corridor

Midhowe broch, one of the largest Iron Age monuments in Orkney. It was built in an easily defended position, with sweeping views acros the sea

Yarso is a good point from which to climb to the top of Ward Hill for a fine view over the North Isles of Westray, Sanday, Eday, Egilsay and Wyre.

Descending from Ward Hill and continuing along the shore westwards brings one to Midhowe cairn, the largest Neolithic burial so far discovered in Britain. In its undisturbed state Midhowe was a large grassy mound, but excavations in 1932–3 showed that it consisted of an oblong drystone structure containing a corridor-like burial chamber, along the sides of which were twenty-four burial stalls divided by sandstone slabs.

Midhowe contained the disarticulated remains of twenty-five individuals, also the bones of oxen, sheep, pigs and red deer. There were few artefacts. So important was this discovery that a large hangar-like structure

was built over it so that it could be left open for inspection. Overhead gangways allow the whole structure to be examined in detail.

Close by is another huge monument, this one dating from the Romano-British period: Midhowe broch, one of the largest structures of its kind; in fact, as its name implies, it is the middle broch of three, the other two remaining unexcavated. Midhowe is particularly well placed for defence, being protected on two sides by deep geos or sea-inlets. Its narrow landward side is protected by a massive double ditch and bank. The first fifteen stairs of the broch tower are preserved, and there is a central well. The chaos of stone slabs inside and outside the broch indicates the usual later domestic additions.

Midhowe broch

St Magnus's church, Egilsay with its unusual round tower, built on the spot where the saint was murdered in 1117

EGILSAY

CROSSING TO EGILSAY brings one to St Magnus' church. This striking building stands on a high point of the island within easy walking distance of the pier; it is said to mark the spot where Earl Magnus was murdered in 1117. The round tower looks as though it may have been designed to an Irish model, but there are no known connections between this island and Ireland.

WYRE

WYRE is a short boat trip from Egilsay, and its Norse castle and church are within easy walking distance of the pier on that island. The castle is mentioned twice in the *Orkneyinga Saga*. It was built by Kolbein Hruga, one of the landed magnates established here in the time of Earl Thorfinn, and dates from the mid-twelfth century.

The small roofless church nearby is an example of the churches built by landowners in the Norse period and retained as their personal property. It has traces of Romanesque work, no doubt influenced by the builders of St Magnus' Cathedral in Kirkwall. Kolbein Hruga's son, Bjarni was an early Bishop of Orkney and a founder of Orcadian education. Kolbein is thought to have built this church at his son's behest.

A Norse castle on Wyre island , built by Kolbein Hruga

SHAPINSAY

ALSO WITHIN EASY REACH of Kirkwall by regular ferry is the low island of Shapinsay, with its fine estate house of Balfour Castle and its 'wood', which is not much more than waist-high because of the wind.

The Balfour estate was one of the first to modernise itself in the mid-nineteenth century, and the great increases in productivity achieved on the Balfour lands soon persuaded the other landowners on Shapinsay to make improvements of their own.

Balfour Castle was built on the site of an earlier house and finished in 1848. The cottages of Balfour village were originally provided for stonemasons working on the castle. The Balfours, who came from Fife, held the Shapinsay estate from 1560 to 1961, after which it passed either to the Zawadski family or to owner-farmers who now farm all the land on the island.

Shapinsay is perhaps Orkney's most intensively farmed island. The tradition of modernisation begun by the Balfours has been continued, so that today the island is noted for the high and sometimes prize-winning quality of its beef cattle and sheep exports.

11 THE FARTHEST ISLANDS

BEYOND ROUSAY, EGILSAY AND WYRE is an outer semi-circle of islands which are very well worth visiting. They may be reached by Orkney Islands Shipping Company (OISC) ferry or Loganair flights from Kirkwall. The North Isles are attractive for many reasons: serious ornithologists will certainly wish to visit some of their notable bird-watching localities – reference has already been made to the superb bird-cliffs at the western end of Westray, extending from Noup Head to Inga Ness; also to the opportunities for observing migrant species around the freshwater lochs and dunes of Eday, Sanday and North Ronaldsay.

The North Isles also have some very fine archaeological sites: Neolithic remains are numerous on Eday, Westray, Papa Westray and Sanday. Sanday was an important population centre in Neolithic times, and was also much favoured by the Norse settlers, who used it as a base for their twice-annual *vikings*, raids to the west and south in spring and after harvest. On Westray, Noltland Castle is a massive monument to the coming of Scots power to Orkney, and also to the fall of the earldom in the tumultuous days of the Stewarts, father and son.

Eighteenth- and nineteenth-century land reforms and farming improvements have left a strong estate imprint upon all the islands; and there are some notable developments from modern times, showing what can be done by enterprising individuals and groups of people to offset the disadvantages of remoteness which afflict the whole of Orkney and the North Isles most of all.

Left: the P&O ferry St Sunniva *passes Noup Head in Westray on her way to Shetland*

Gun-ports in the massive walls of Noltland Castle, Westray. The castle is a monument to sixteenth century misrule and extortion of the island's people by a Scottish laird

Noltland Castle in Westray, a massive stronghold built by Gilbert Balfour around 1560. Balfour was one of the most unsavoury lairds who ever ruled in Orkney. He was eventually executed in Sweden for various acts of subversion

Cross Kirk in Westray, dating from the Norse period

PAPA WESTRAY

PAPA WESTRAY is a microcosm of Orkney; it is linked with Westray by the world's shortest scheduled flight. At the north end of the island is one of Orkney's most important archaeological sites, the Knap of Howar, a hut cluster similar to Skara Brae, but older. Its houses are believed to be the oldest standing domestic structures in Europe, roughly 5,000 years of age. Here also are the remains of a Celtic monastery; while the very name of the island reminds us of the presence of *papae*, fathers of the Celtic church. All *pap* names have this meaning.

Place-names and the style of old houses are both monuments to the Norse settlement. Holland House is a large estate-owner's mansion, begun by the Traill family soon after the union with Scotland and occupied by them for three hundred years. Finally there is a modern economy, based on farming and a little fishing, and notable for the pioneer development of a co-operative which not only supports farmers, but also provides a wide range of services to residents and visitors. This cooperative is regarded as a model for collaborative developments in small communities everywhere; it was started with help from the Highlands and Islands Development Board (HIDB) in 1978.

SANDAY

SANDAY is a low-lying island with sand-dunes and sweeping empty beaches; it reaches far out into the open sea and has long been a notable place for ship-wrecks. It is also a prime locality for watching migrant birds in spring and autumn. Ducks, waders, corncrakes, grey plovers,

Farm buildings and the house at Stove are reminders of nineteenth-century farm improvements in Sanday

knots, sanderlings, bar-tailed godwits, turnstones, chats, flycatchers, warblers, red-backed shrikes and wrynecks all visit the island with remarkable frequency, blown off their continental course by strong winds. In autumn, great skeins of greylag and pink-footed geese fly past en route from Iceland and are a splendid spectacle. There is an abundance of the more usual seabirds around the shore, and many seals and otters.

Sanday has always been an important farming island – for centuries it was the granary of Orkney; today it concentrates on beef production like the rest of the county. There is a local fishing industry too, which provides lobsters, crabs and scallops for the Kirkwall market. Sanday is also noted for its knitwear, organised on a cooperative basis; and surprisingly there is a small electronics factory, founded by an inventor to exploit certain niches in the global electronics market.

Silhouette, Elsness. Sanday is one of the flattest, as well as the most fertile of the north isles

NORTH RONALDSAY

NORTH RONALDSAY is even further out and lower-lying than Sanday. Coming to it from the sea, one has the impression of a few farms and a lighthouse standing in the waves; closer inspection reveals that there is in fact a little firm land around them. Less than a hundred people now live on Orkney's farthest island. The lighthouse is the tallest in Britain and a reminder that this small island has had more shipwrecks even than Sanday. The lighthouse is one of the last to be manned, and is to be automated in 1998.

The island has two unique features, its dyke and its sheep. A stone-built dyke completely encircles the island, following the shore, its function to confine flocks of pre-historic sheep to the foreshore where they eat seaweed; only at lambing time are the ewes brought inland. Shearing and dipping are carried out as a communal activity, and there are eleven enclosures around the coasts into which the sheep are gathered. The days of this traditional form of sheep husbandry are clearly numbered, however, as it is labour-intensive and not very profitable. In late 1990 the coastal dyke was badly breached by storm waves and repairs proved difficult and costly; eventually repairs are likely to exceed the capacity of the community on North Ronaldsay to carry them out.

At the south end of the island is an important group of Iron Age and later domestic structures associated with the broch of Burrian – this seems to have been an important settlement in Pictish times. Here the Burrian cross was found, a slab of stone inscribed with a symbol which has since been used widely as a motif in Orcadian jewellery. Burrian is a site to be visited if at all possible.

EDAY

EDAY is very different from the other North Isles in that it has extensive areas of heather moorland, rich in peat; these moors support Orkney's only regularly breeding whimbrel. The moors terminate in fine bird-cliffs facing the Atlantic. The eastern side of the island is fertile and low-lying. In this island, too, there are numerous Neolithic sites, concentrated on the northern uplands and its appendage, the tiny Calf of Eday.

Visitors who fly into Eday will land at London airport, the only *airport* of that name in Britain!

STRONSAY

STRONSAY has a recent history different from all the other North Isles. The village of Whitehall, where the ferry arrives, looks like a fishing village imported from the east coast of Scotland; and this is almost what it is. It came into existence in the great days of the herring fisheries at the beginning of the nineteenth century. Then, more than three hundred drifters would tie-up here each season, supported by a small army of herring-gutting and-barrelling 'lassies' who were housed in a barracks built on nearby Papa Stronsay. The great days of herring lasted until the 1930s, after which over-fishing or changes in the behaviour of the shoals caused a gradual decline. Whitehall then suffered the same fate as ports all along the North Sea coast, such as Buckie, Scarborough, Great Yarmouth and Lowestoft. Most of the buildings associated with the fishery – such as curing houses – have gone, but one curious relic does remain: the wreck of a concrete barge built in France about 1900 and used to bring coal to Orkney to bunker the herring fleet. It lies off Whitehall in Franks Bay.

TANGLES ON THE SHORE

The variety of seaweed called kelp has long been important in Orkney; in medieval and possibly even more ancient times it was used untreated to fertilise the fields, and was sometimes dried and burned for domestic fuel. In the mid-eighteenth century kelp became a valuable export, used in the production of soap, glass and iodine; today it is still gathered by numerous collectors for shipment to a factory in Oban – Sanday and the other North Isles are good places to see it drying on racks along the shore. It is now used in the production of stabilisers and emulsifiers in the food industry, and also as a gelling agent in pet-foods. Moreover it has an increasing number of applications in the textile-printing and pharmaceutical industries.

Whitehall, the nineteenth century
village built to service the herring trade

At the north end of Whitehall village is the well of Kildinguie, an ancient holy well whose waters were reputed to cure all ills save the black death. Pilgrims came here to drink the waters century by century; a few come still, though the waters do not look inviting. Stronsay was a 'holy isle' in the pre-Norse period, with several monastic sites in precipitous locations along its east coast.

Like the other North Isles, Stronsay has many excellent bird-watching sites, and also a range of archaeological remains, most of which await detailed investigation. On its cliffed eastern coast is Orkney's finest natural arch, the Vat of Kirbister. Its paramount position is assured now that the splendid arch at Yesnaby in West Mainland has fallen, smashed one night by a great winter storm. Kirbister arch will fall sometime too, next year or a hundred years from now.

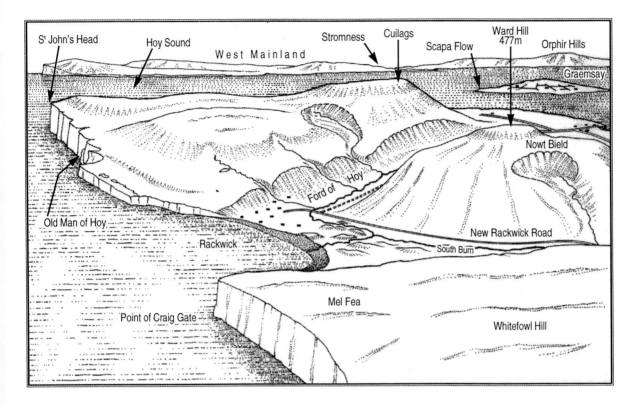

S¹ John's Head — Hoy Sound — West Mainland — Stromness — Cuilags — Scapa Flow — Ward Hill 477m — Orphir Hills — Graemsay — Nowt Bield — Old Man of Hoy — Ford of Hoy — New Rackwick Road — Rackwick — South Burn — Mel Fea — Point of Craig Gate — Whitefowl Hill

12 A WALK IN NORTH HOY

THE WALK FROM MO NESS PIER in north-east Hoy through to the Atlantic coast must surely rank as one of Britain's greatest hill and coastal walks. It can be accomplished in one day, but those who have the time may well decide to stay in Hoy itself and explore this magnificent area in more detail.

Mo Ness pier may be reached by ferry from Stromness or by arrangement with a private boatman; the Orkney Tourist Board will advise about up-to-the-minute arrangements. The crossing takes about 45 minutes and it is advisable to be landed at Mo Ness pier not later than 10 o'clock; a pick-up at 5 o'clock will then give enough time for the walk, provided one keeps going.

The farmland around Mo Ness is an area of surviving estate land, a form of land management which once dominated the whole of Orkney. Some conifer planting has been attempted here in the shelter of the Hoy hills, but only with moderate success; salt-laden wind is, of course, the great enemy of trees and this area is not completely sheltered.

As one walks inland from the pier, the hill to the left is Ward Hill, the highest point in the islands. The name indicates that a beacon was sited here in Norse times, and it was used as recently as the Napoleonic wars.

The summit of Ward Hill. The broken stony surface is evidence of arctic conditions in winter

Top: North Hoy

The energetic may like to scramble to the summit, which affords tremendous views over the whole of Orkney. To the west the coast of Sutherland is visible almost as far as Cape Wrath, while inland are the great peaks of Ben Loyal, Ben Hope and Ben Klibreck, the most remote of all Scotland's high peaks. The summit of Ward Hill is a rocky 'pavement' of stones, the result of arctic conditions which occur on high ground in this latitude.

The Old Man of Hoy, with the Scrabster – Stromness ferry in the distance

The right-hand hill is the Cuilags, not quite as high as Ward Hill but offering more extensive walking and equally splendid views. A track past the reservoir, Sandy Loch, leads through a splendid glacial valley to the Atlantic coast at Rackwick. Rackwick is reminiscent of Shetland, being the only example of a completely decayed crofting township on estate land where most of the houses are still in place. There are fine examples of longhouses, some of which have lately been turned into holiday homes. There is also a self-catering hostel which makes a good base for exploring the area. Rackwick is the Orkney home of Sir Peter Maxwell Davies, Orkney's most distinguished composer and a prime mover in the annual St Magnus' Festival.

North-west from Rackwick, a track leads to the cliff-top and on towards the Old Man of Hoy. The 'head' of this remarkable feature comes into view from afar as one approaches across an area of open moorland where Arctic hares may be seen (these are a relatively recent introduction). Here also the walker is likely to face some determined dive-bombing by skuas (bonxies) which regard this as their territory—it is highly advisable to wear a hat and to hold a walking stick above one's head.

Right: Brae Brough cliffs, looking north. The tiny speck near the top of the picture is the ferry, revealing the scale of these giant cliffs

From the cliff edge, the Old Man is fully revealed. 'He' consists of a red sandstone pillar the height of St Paul's Cathedral, standing on a solidified flow of black volcanic lava. This hard lava foundation preserves the pillar from rapid destruction by the waves.

The Old Man is almost certainly a quite modern feature of the coast. When Murdoch Mackenzie made his first accurate sea-charts of Orkney in the 1750s, sketching in important features of the coast, he indicated a small promontory at this point. In 1815, when William Daniell visited this spot and produced his splendid aquatint, he showed an Old Man which was much more massive than today, with a cave through its base. All coastal features such as the Old Man sea-stack are temporary; no one knows when the next major collapse will occur, and it may well be that visitors next year, or a century hence, will come to this point and find that the Old Man is no more, demolished by some great winter storm.

Beyond the Old Man, the walk follows the rising cliff-top to reach the summit of Britain's highest vertical cliffs at Brae Brough. The magnificence of these red, ochre and brown cliffs has to be seen to be believed. Photographers should try to include a fishing boat in their pictures as an indication of scale, otherwise the sheer size of these giant cliffs will be lost.

From Brae Brough, it is a relatively short climb to the Cuilags summit, and on a clear day this is a place to linger and consider the long and stirring history which has unfolded around the shores of Scapa Flow, laid out like a map below. In the north face of the Cuilags there is a fine corrie, to which golden eagles have returned after a long absence.

From the Cuilags summit, follow the ridge-top until it ends in a steep descent to Sandy Loch and so back to Mo Ness pier.

To savour the full quality of this walk, the well-equipped, energetic and experienced should attempt it in winter. On a fine, icy, brilliantly clear day, visibility can be unlimited and the view immense.

The Old Man seen from the north

Useful information and places to visit

Kirkwall

Orkney Tourist Office, 6 Broad Street, Kirkwall, KW15 1NX
First and essential port of call for all visitors. Information, bookings, hours of admission, small museum. Open all year. Tel: 01856 872856.

St Magnus' Cathedral
Founded 1137. Open Monday to Saturday, Church of Scotland services Sunday. Admission free. Concerts.

Bishop's Palace
Twelfth century and Earl's Palace, early seventeenth century, both in care of Historic Scotland. Standard HS hours, admission charge.

Tankerness House Museum, opposite cathedral
Splendid museum of Orcadian prehistory and history; garden. Open daily all year, admission charge April to September, garden free.

Orkney Library, Laing Street
Founded 1683, Scotland's oldest public library. Orkney Room has superb collection of Orkney books and maps. Tel: 01856 873166.

Orkney Arts Theatre
See posters for dramatic, operatic, musical events and conferences.

Highland Park Distillery
Northernmost whisky distillery, situated towards airport. Guided tours available weekdays.

Shops
Kirkwall's main street has a remarkable range of interesting, high quality shops. See for example Ola Gorie, jewellery; Ortak jewellery; Judith Glue, distinctive knitwear; also art galleries, bookshops, shops selling local cheeses and other foodstuffs.

Stromness

Orkney Tourist Office at Pierhead; small office, subsidiary to Kirkwall. Tel: 01856 850716.

Pier Arts Centre
Attractive modern art galley, situated in converted eighteenth-century house. Permanent collection, exhibitions, open all year, admission free.

Stromness Museum
Orkney natural and maritime history, including fossils, birds, butterflies and moths, fishing, whaling, the Hudson's Bay Company and the German fleet scuttled in Scapa Flow. Open all year, admission charge.

Stromness Library
Close to natural history Museum. Founded 1905, fine local collection.

West Mainland

Maes Howe
Finest Neolithic chambered tomb in Western Europe, with largest known collection of Norse runic writing. In care of Historic Scotland, standard HS hours, guided visits, admission charge.

Stones of Stenness and Ring of Brodgar
Notable henge monuments dating from third millennium BC. Open sites, north of main Kirkwall–Stromness road.

Skara Brae, Bay of Skaill
The best-preserved Neolithic 'village' in Europe, dating from around 3000 BC. In care of Historic Scotland. Standard HS hours, admission charge.

Brough of Birsay, north-west Mainland
Tidal island, access by causeway; check tide times with Tourist Office or in *Orcadian* newspaper. Major Norse remains, with signs of older structures, perhaps ecclesiastical. In care of Historic Scotland, free access.

Broch of Gurness, Aikerness
Massive remains of Iron Age fortified tower, with domestic structures, some Norse. In care of Historic Scotland. Normal HS hours. Admission charge.

Round Church, Orphir
Apse of a Norse-age round church, only example in Scotland. Location overlooking Orphir Bay, south of main road from Scapa to Stromness. Open access. Remains of a Norse earl's drinking hall nearby.

Earl's Palace, Birsay
Late sixteenth century, ruinous structure, in care of Historic Scotland. Open access.

Kirbuster Farm Museum (Orkney Farm & Folk Museum)
Located at east end of Boardhouse Loch. A remarkable

survival of a traditional Orkney 'firehoose' with central hearth and stone bed. Restored Victorian garden. Open daily March to October.

Corrigall Farm Museum (Orkney Farm & Folk Museum)
Located in central West Mainland south-east of Dounby. An elaborate late-nineteenth century farmhouse and parallel outbuilding, comprising byre, barn, threshing floor and kiln. A notable restoration by Orkney Islands Council and a 'must' for all visitors interested in rural country life in the immediate pre-modern period. Open daily March to October. Admission charge.

Fursbeck Pottery, Harray
Located in former school south of Dounby. Distinctive stylish pottery, also watercolours, bird paintings by D.S. Harris.

HOY AND WALLS

Lyness Naval Base
Museum devoted to the Royal Navy's connections with Scapa Flow in two world wars. Interpretation centre, with admission charge. Also Royal Navy cemetery.

Martello towers, Longhope
Built 1813 to protect Baltic convoys from United States naval and private raiders. South tower open to public.

Dwarfie Stane, north Hoy
Only known example in Britain of a rock-hewn Neolithic tomb. Located under the hill south of the Mo Ness to Rackwick Road.

EAST MAINLAND AND THE EASTERN SOUTH ISLES

Brough of Deerness
Eastern tip of Mainland. Precipitous rocky islet, with ruin of a possibly Celtic chapel. Fine coastal walks.

Graemeshall
Nineteenth-century Scottish laird's house, now containing a notable private antiques collection. Limited hours, admission charge.

Italian chapel, Lamb Holm
Built by Italian prisoners-of-war during World War II. Open daily, Roman Catholic service on Sundays: see notices.

Orkney Fossil and Vintage Centre, Burray
Private museum of Orkney geology, beautifully presented by enthusiasts. Admission charge, shop and restaurant.

St Margaret's Hope
Small town which originated as a nineteenth-century fishing station. Name derives from Margaret, Maid of Norway, betrothed to King Alexander of Scotland; she died here in 1290 aged seven years. Smiddy museum is a village blacksmith's collection of horse-drawn farm implements. Admission charge. Wireless museum illustrates aspects of wartime communications from 1930s onwards. Open April to September. Admission charge.

Isbister: Tomb of the Eagles
Recently excavated Neolithic tomb and other structures. Museum in which exhibits may be handled. Explanation and debate. Admission charge. This is Orkney's most thought-provoking archaeological visit. Location near far southern tip of South Ronaldsay. Follow signposts.

NORTH ISLES

Rousay, south shore
Midhowe stalled Neolithic cairn, huge stone-built 'ship of death'. Other notable cairns nearby. Midhowe Iron Age broch, very large example. Open access to broch. Check access to locked cairns with Tourist Office.

Egilsay
St Magnus' church, site of Earl Magnus' murder in the early twelfth century. Round tower looks Irish but there are no known Irish connections. Open access.

Wyre
Norse castle, the oldest in Scotland, built by Kolbein Hruga or 'Cubbie Roo'. Open access.

Westray
Noup Head bird cliffs.
Peirowall, Orkney's finest natural harbour and probable site of a major Norse trading settlement. The name used to be simply Wall – 'the bay'.
Noltland (pronounced Noutland) castle, stronghold of megalomaniac Scottish proprietor, Gilbert Balfour. Restoration by Historic Scotland. Key at nearby farm.

Papa Westray
Knap of Howar, oldest-known domestic structure in Europe, begun 1100 years before Egypt's great pyramid.

North Ronaldsay
Sea wall, which encloses the island and keeps the ancient breed of sheep on the beach. Recently damaged by storm waves.
Old beacon, lit in 1789 to try to prevent shipwrecks; there were sixteen between 1773 and 1788.

PLACE-NAMES AND THEIR PRONUNCIATION

THE INTERPRETATION of place-names is fraught with difficulties. Modern forms of place-names in Britain have often been arrived at through centuries of modification. They have sometimes involved changes of language, and many have reached their present forms as a result of Ordnance Survey field-workers writing down what they thought local people with strong regional accents told them about the names of hills, rivers and farms.

In Orkney there have been three major language changes, from a hypothetical Celtic language spoken by the First Orcadians, through a colonial form of Old Norse down to Lowland Scots. Most names are of Norse origin, but some must surely incorporate Celtic elements; usually we cannot be sure which these are. Difficulties of interpretation are made worse by the lack of early documentary evidence. In England, early forms of place-names were written down by William the Conqueror's surveyors in *Domesday Book*, the taxation inventory made in 1086. These early forms often allow us to understand what modern names mean. In Orkney, no comparable early record exists. The *Orkneyinga Saga*, which does mention some place-names, was written down in Iceland centuries after it had been composed and declaimed in Orkney. Other written sources, such as rentals, came very much later. The interpretation of Orcadian place-names must therefore be approached with extreme caution.

An example will show the difficulties. The -wall in Kirkwall, the capital, has nothing to do with walls or boundaries. It derives from the Old Norse either for a bay or a field; without further evidence one cannot tell which. Fortunately in this case Kirkwall is mentioned in the *Saga* and we can be sure its name means 'Church Bay'.

With this preliminary warning, the probable meanings of some of the commoner place names will be discussed, beginning with the name 'Orkney' itself.

ORKNEY

THIS IS CERTAINLY a pre-Norse name, having been recorded by the Latin writer Diodorus Siculus at about the time of Julius Caesar's invasion of Britain, when the geography of the country was being investigated. It probably commemorates the name of a Celtic tribal group which lived in the islands and had the wild boar as its emblem.

Overleaf: Hoy seen from Brinkies Brae above Stromness, where Orkney's oldest rocks reach the surface

ISLAND NAMES

MAINLAND, the name of Orkney's principal island, is relatively modern. It replaced the Norse *Hrossey*, 'horse island', which goes back to *Saga* times. The name *Pomona*, given to Mainland on some early maps and even on the occasional inaccurate modern map, has never been used by Orcadians, nor indeed by anyone else. It arose from a literary error, the mis-translation of a Latin text into Scots in seventeenth-century Denmark.

Beginning in the south-west and moving clockwise around Scapa Flow, Hoy is the 'high island', contrasting with Flotta, the 'flat island'. Burray is 'broch island'; it has at least three broch sites. South Ronaldsay takes its name from a Norse colonist named Rognvald. Lamb Holm (pronounced 'ham'), site of the Italian chapel, records the name of a Norse settler Lambi. To the south, Swona is 'pig island', Stroma the island in the stream or tidal race of the Pentland (Pict-land) Firth.

North of Mainland, Rousay is Rolfe's island, Eday the isthmus island and Egilsay Egill's island. Wyre means 'arrow-head', which neatly describes its shape. Sanday is the sandy island, Westray the western-most island. The meanings of Stronsay and Shapinsay are both uncertain, though the former may incorporate a Norse settler's name.

NATURAL FEATURES

BEING NAVIGATORS, the Norwegians who settled in Orkney took a very close interest in the physical features of the coast, especially those which helped them to sail safely in fog and wild weather. They gave a multitude of names to Orkney's rocks, cliffs, bays, caves and headlands, many of which are now quite forgotten; but the modern map still shows many examples of nesses or headlands, ayres or sandbars, oyces (pronounced 'yousses') or river mouths, geos or deeply-cut rocky inlets, gloups or blow-holes, wicks and walls which both mean bays and reefs or exposed rocks, likely causes of shipwreck.

To give some examples: Stromness takes its name from the headland which juts out into the fierce tidal stream of Hoy Sound. In Kirkwall, the Ayre Hotel stands beside the barrier of sand and shingle which shuts off the Peerie or Little Sea from the sea proper. The water from that 'sea' drains through the oyce next to the former egg-packing station, now turned into offices. Ayres or sandbars give the Bay of Ireland near Stromness its name. It is sandbar bay and has nothing to do with the country of Ireland.

Inland, the many Ward Hills, one on almost every island, record the sites of Norse beacon fires, used to mobilise the islanders against invasion. The main beacons were used right down to modern times and were also an invaluable aid to mapmakers from the seventeenth century onwards. More generally, hills are called feas, derived from the Norse *fjell*, fell in northern England.

Streams in Orkney are burns and never becks. Some stream names incorporate the Norse element -a, meaning water. Streams often take their names from an important house nearby and run through valleys called dales. Orkney dales are often very small-scale features, though Summerdale in west Mainland is a broad and open valley comparable in size to a Yorkshire dale. Chun is the Orcadian version of tarn or small fresh-water loch. Hope means bay, as in St Margaret's Hope; it may be modified to Whup, Hubbit or Hubbin, almost unrecognisable as the same word.

FARM NAMES

THE COMMONEST FARM NAMES end in some form of -bister, -bist or -buster, the Old Norse word for a farm. Names with the ending -setter simply mean dwellings and have no connection with the Norwegian *saeter*, a high summer grazing. Skaill indicates a very important property in Norse times, as does Bu, the home of a principal landowner, sometimes an earl. Quoys were secondary farms on the edges of the initial Norse settlements. In Stromness, though, they indicate long, narrow properties extending inland from a landing-place. Names ending in -ston derive from another Norse word for farmstead and are thought to indicate a relatively late settlement phase.

Place-names have been added to Orkney's landscape layer upon layer. In addition to those of Celtic and Norse origin, there are names such as Balfour in Shapinsay and Carrick in Eday which record the arrival of estate owners from Scotland after the union of 1468. The modernisation and extension of many Orkney estates in the late eighteenth and nineteenth centuries produced farm names such as Park Hall, Newburgh, New Place and Newhouse; while connections between Orcadians and faraway places in the British Empire are commemorated in names such as Madras and Lucknow, Canada West and Virginia. Crimean War battle names such as Balaclava and Inkerman tell us that farms were established around 1853–6.

Visitors to Orkney who are interested in place-name interpretation are recommended first to go out with the Ordnance map and look at the country. Many names describe the lie of the land or some distinctive feature of a settlement site and their meanings can be worked out, or at least guessed at, through direct observation. Those who wish to take the study further should begin by consulting the late Hugh Marwick's masterly *Orkney Farm Names* (Kirkwall Press, 1952) and *The Place Names of Birsay* (Aberdeen University Press, 1970). In this second book, dealing with just one parish in north-west Mainland, Marwick discusses more than 600 names. This is an indication of the size of the task still to be done in extracting the full story from Orkney's place-names.

ACKNOWLEDGEMENTS

MANY PEOPLE have helped me to write this book. In particular I wish to thank Dr Philip Wheeler of Nottingham University and the Geographical Field Group who introduced me to Orkney in 1960. Elaine Bullard MBE, Orkney's distinguished naturalist and President of Orkney Field Club, has always been instant with good advice. She and other members of the OFC, notably the late John Scott of Onston, have taught me much about Orkney. The late Evan Macgillivray MBE, when County Librarian, talked me into the Orkney of the Sagas; his successors in that notable library have been of great help ever since. The late Ernest Marwick, member of a long line of fine Orcadian scholars, was an inspiration. Orcadians who have simply talked about their islands and students who have worked with me in Orkney have all helped to bring this book to fruition.

FURTHER READING

Anderson, P.D. *Black Patie; the life and times of Patrick Stewart Earl of Orkney, Lord of Shetland* (John Donald Publishers, 1992)

Bailey, P. *Orkney* (David & Charles, 1971, 1985)

Balfour, E. *Orkney Birds: Status and Guide* (Stromness, 1972)

Brown, G.M. *An Orkney Tapestry* (Gollancz 1969)

Brown, G.M. *Vinland* (Murray, 1992)

Bullard, E.R. *Orkney: A Checklist of Vascular Plants, Flowering Plants and Ferns* (Stromness, 1975)

Childe, V. Gordon *Skara Brae: A Pictish Village in Orkney* (Kegan Paul, Trench, Trubner, 1931)

Clarke, D.V. *The Neolithic Village at Skara Brae, Orkney, Excavations 1972-3; An interim report* (Kirkwall Press, 1976)

Clouston, J. Storer The Orkney Parishes (W.R. Mackintosh, *The Orcadian*, 1927)

Clouston, J. Storer History of Orkney (W.R. Mackintosh, *The Orcadian*, 1932)

Drever, W.P. *Udal Law and the Foreshore* (Kirkwall, 1914)

Drever, W.P. *Udal Law in the Orkneys and Zetland* (Kirkwall, 1914)

Elliot, R.W.V. *Runes* (Manchester, 1959)

Fereday, R.P. *The Longhope Battery and Towers* (W.R. Rendall, 1971)

Firth, H. *The Ancient Settlement of the North* (The Orkney Press, 1994)

Firth, J. *Reminiscences of an Orkney Parish* (W.R. Rendall, 1922, reprinted 1972)

Graham-Campbell, J. & Kidd, D. *The Vikings* (British Museum Publications, 1980)

Gorrie, D. *Summers and Winters in the Orkneys* (Simpkin, Marshall & Co, 1868)

Groundwater, W. *Birds and Mammals of Orkney* (Kirkwall Press, 1974)

Hedges, J.W. *Tomb of the Eagles; a window on stone age tribal Britain (*Murray, 1984)

Hewison, W.S. *This great harbour; Scapa Flow.* (The Orkney Press, 1985, 1990)

Highlands and Islands Enterprise *Sustainable Tourism in Europe – an Orkney Case Study* (Edinburgh, 1994 – a resource pack for schools)

Hossack B.H. *Kirkwall in the Orkneys (*William Peace, 1900)

Jackson, A. *The Pictish Trail* (The Orkney Press, 1989)

Jackson, A. *The Symbol Stones of Scotland* (The Orkney Press, 1990)

Linklater, E. *The Ultimate Viking* (Macmillan, 1955)

Linklater, E. *The Man on my Back* (Macmillan, 1941)

Mackenzie, M. *Orcades: or a Geographic and Hydrographic Survey of the Orkney and Lewis Islands in Eight Maps* (London, 1776)

Mackintosh, W.R. Around the Orkney Peat Fires (W.R. Mackintosh, *The Orcadian*, 1914)

Marwick, E.W. *The Folklore of Orkney and Shetland* (London, 1975)

Marwick, H. *The Orkney Norn* (Oxford University Press, 1926)

Marwick, H. *Orkney* (Robert Hale, 1951)

Meek, E. *Islands of Birds* (RSPB, 1985)

Miller, R. *Orkney* (Batsford, 1976)

Miller, R. *The County of Orkney* (Scottish Academic Press, 1985)

Mooney, J. St Magnus, Earl of Orkney (W.R. Mackintosh, *The Orcadian*, 1935)

Mooney, J. The Cathedral and Royal Burgh of Kirkwall (W.R. Mackintosh, *The Orcadian*, 1943)

Pállson, H. & Edwards, P. (eds) *Orkneyinga Saga* (Hogarth Press, 1978)

Rendall, R. *Mollusca Orcadiensis* (Kirkwall Press, 1956)

Rendall, R. *Orkney Shore* (Kirkwall Press, 1960)

Renfrew, C. *Investigations in Orkney* (Thames & Hudson, 1979)

Renfrew, C. (ed) *The Prehistory of Orkney* (Edinburgh University Press, 1990, 1994)

Ritchie, A. *Exploring Scotland's Heritage; Orkney and Shetland* (HMSO, 1985)

Ritchie, A. *Picts* (HMSO, 1989)

Ritchie, A. *Viking Scotland* (Batsford, 1993)

Ritchie, A. & G. *The Ancient Monuments of Orkney* (HMSO, 1978)

Robertson, J. *Uppies and Doonies* (Kirkwall Press, 1968)

Robertson, J.D.M. *An Orkney anthology; the selected works of Ernest Walker Marwick, Volume 1* (Scottish Academic Press, 1991)

Royal Commission on the Ancient Monuments of Scotland, 3 vols (HMSO, 1946)

Shearer, J., Groundwater, W. & Mackay, J.D. *The New Orkney Book* (Nelson, 1966)

Spence, M. *Flora Orcadiensis* (Kirkwall Press, 1914)

Tait, C. *The Orkney Guide Book* (Kirkwall Press, 1991)

Taylor, A.B. (ed) *Orkneyinga Saga* (Oliver & Boyd, 1938)

Thomson, W.P. *History of Orkney* (Mercat Press, 1987)

Troup, J.A. & Eunson, F. *Stromness* (Stromness, 1967)

Wadham, S.P. & Casarini, M.P. Signs of Life (recent investigation into the fate of the Franklin expedition) *Geographical*, LXVI, No 4, 1994, pp 26–27

Wainwright, F.T. (ed) *The Problem of the Picts* (Nelson, 1955)

Wainwright, F.T. (ed) *The Northern Isles* (Nelson, 1962)

INDEX

Page numbers in italic indicate illustrations